I never write reviews...

Watching Peter Pru and Empire Builders' YouTube videos alone allowed me to make $3K, compared to a year with Shopify "gurus" and their courses (which were not as in-depth as they should have been). I truly believe Peter Pru does everything to the highest standard. And I love his motto: Keep it stupid simple, make a start, and work on your business (not *in* your business). Love, love, love the content! This is the first time I have ever personally done over $1K per month in ecommerce...and this is just the testing phase.

— Nana W.

I've been making $20K/month for the last 3 months.

Ecommerce Empire Academy opened my eyes to new opportunities. Peter and his training not only showed me how to make money and create amazing products that solve real problems, but also how to think like an entrepreneur. I highly recommend going over Peter's material. I've been making $20K per month for the last three months, and that wouldn't be possible without Peter's mentorship.

— Javier G.

Amazing content

When I got Peter's course, I knew nothing about selling online. I love how he breaks it down so even I can understand it. My favorite thing about my experience with him is that he always puts himself out there to help as often as he can, from personally answering questions to solving new problems and sharing before you run into them. It is the best investment in myself I have ever made.

— Jerry W.

Great team to work with!

I have been working with Peter and his team for over a year, and I couldn't be happier with the experience I have had! They have been extremely helpful, knowledgeable, and encouraging along the way and have guided me to a six-figure business. I had the pleasure of getting to work with them in person a few months ago, and it was very clear they are all genuine, down-to-earth guys who truly wanted me to succeed. I would highly recommend them to anyone looking to grow a business!

— **Shannon J.**

Excellent! Helped me scale to 6 figures

Peter and the rest of the team were a huge help in getting my business off the ground. The Ecommerce Empire Builders course lays out what you need to know from A to Z to start and run a successful ecommerce business. Taking this course will dramatically cut your learning curve and save you hundreds of hours. Over time, the course will pay for itself many times over. It is well worth the investment.

— **Anthony B.**

The longer you wait, the more time and money you waste

Prior to joining, I always asked myself why ecommerce course creators make courses. Aren't they too busy with their own "successful" business? The answer is they found a way to do something they love: teach others. You will see that they genuinely want you to succeed. You can see their pride when a student hits their own goals.

— **Viet H.**

Peter opened my eyes

Peter's Ecommerce Empire Builders course opened my eyes up to what I was missing and what I didn't even know to think about. I had tried to figure out the whole ecommerce puzzle for years, but it wasn't until Peter's course that I learned how to think differently. With the proper guidance and a lot of hard work, I was able to take my business from $0 to $50K a month. I recommend Peter's course, but only for those serious about putting in the work to make it happen. He's great at what he does, great at teaching it, and the EEB team is top-notch. Keep up the great work, Peter!

— **Phil B.**

If you don't want to lose money, time, and energy, then get this program

Game changer of a program! I researched many leaders in the ecommerce industry, and everyone was always tagging Peter Pru. Now I know why they did. His program is just so in-depth and takes you through every little bit of detail to never leave you in the dust. I was pretty skeptical about the program at first and wasn't sure if the money was worth it, but it has all paid off. Peter's teachings are exactly what you need to build a profitable ecommerce business using sales funnels. 5/5

— **Michael F.**

I've been working with Peter for 3 years

I've been working with Peter for the past three years. Within the first year, I was able to leave my job. If you're looking to join or you're on the fence, I understand—I was in that position too. Peter has over 10 years of experience in the industry, so you have nothing to lose but everything to gain. Take a chance on yourself—you're worth it. I'll see you on the inside!

— **Bronson T.**

Changed my life for the better

Ecommerce Empire Builders has changed my life for the better. Not long ago, I was working a nine-to-five job where I was constantly stressed and stuck in my position with no room to grow. When I saw Peter Pru on a YouTube ad, I was immediately intrigued. After a few months, I was able to quit my job and earn even more than I had been. I highly recommend this course. You do have to put effort into the learning and be proactive, but it's totally worth it. I am amazed and happy with Ecommerce Empire Builders.

— Arturo R.

AMAZING!

Peter has so much value to give to you in this course. The one thing I really love is that it's evergreen and there is new value being thrown out every week! The community is one of the best around when it comes to asking questions and showing love. Whether you are just starting out or have made some money online already, Peter is the man and he will teach you how to grow and hit your goals! Make the investment in yourself and you will make your money back! Thanks for everything, Pete!

— DJ W.

The strategy and tools needed to get results and change your life

Empire Builders is the real deal. If you do the work, you will end up wealthy. Peter has been a mentor for a few years and has helped me transform myself from making $0 to over $50K per month using the strategies that he teaches.

— Steve S.

ECOMMERCE EMPIRE

THE DEFINITIVE GUIDE TO STARTING & SCALING A FUTURE-PROOF ONLINE BUSINESS

PETER PRU

Copyright © 2021 by Peter Pru

All rights reserved. No part of this publication may be reproduced, distributed, or transmitted in any form or by any means, including photocopying, recording, or other electronic or mechanical methods, without the prior written permission of the publisher, except in the case of brief questions embodied in critical reviews and certain other noncommercial uses permitted by copy law. For permission requests, write to the publisher at the address below.

Ecommerce Press
http://ecommerceempirebuilders.com/

Print ISBN: 978-1-7362309-0-9
Hardcover ISBN: 978-1-7362309-3-0
Ebook ISBN: 978-1-7362309-2-3

Cover Design by Eled Cernik
Interior Layout by Amit Dey
Editing by Julie Willson
Index by Valerie Haynes Perry

Publisher's Cataloging-In-Publication Data
(Prepared by The Donohue Group, Inc.)

Names: Pru, Peter, author.
Title: Ecommerce empire : start and scale your own online business / Peter Pru.
Description: [Philadelphia, Pennsylvania] : Ecommerce Press, [2021]
Identifiers: ISBN 9781736230909 (print) | ISBN 9781736230923 (ebook)
Subjects: LCSH: Electronic commerce. | Selling. | Entrepreneurship. | Success in business.
Classification: LCC HF5548.32 .P78 2021 (print) | LCC HF5548.32 (ebook) | DDC 658.8/72--dc23

To all the Empire Builders who refuse to settle—
Your empire starts now!

CONTENTS

Introduction: Low-Risk, Low-Cost Ecommerce xi
Chapter 1: The Empire Builder's Mindset 1
Chapter 2: Find The Right Niche 19
Chapter 3: Uncover Your Niche 31
Chapter 4: Choose Your Product 45
Chapter 5: Source Your Product 65
Chapter 6: Design Your Sales Funnel 77
Chapter 7: Drive Traffic To Your Funnel 125
Chapter 8: Manage Your Workflow 147
Chapter 9: Build Your Ecommerce Empire 155
Chapter 10: Your Empire Starts Now .165
References 167
Acknowledgements 169
Glossary 171
About The Author 177
Index 179

INTRODUCTION

LOW-RISK, LOW-COST ECOMMERCE

It took me 10 years to become an overnight success story in ecommerce. Yeah it's a cheesy joke, but for those of you who are living in that time, that space between Day One and success—it's real.

You are toiling away, trying to decide how much energy, money, and time to invest, but facing uncertainty over whether you will actually find it on the other side. You are feeling what it's like to try and throw something out there, only to have a few small wins and a lot of big failures. After all, it's only obvious that "it was all worth it" once you come out the other side.

But you're not on the other side...not yet. Maybe you've taken a step or are contemplating dipping a toe into ecommerce.

In 2008, I got into it as a freshman at LaSalle University, where I studied computer science. Twelve years later, I'm the owner of multiple online businesses, which generate millions of dollars every year. I have built over 50 different sales funnels for my students in Ecommerce Empire Builders, and have dedicated the last four years of my life to teaching everyday people how to grow their own Ecommerce Empires.

Most importantly, I get to show folks that they really can have whatever kind of life they want, whether that means a few thousand extra bucks a month, the financial security to quit their job, or the tools to build a legacy business they can leave to their children.

I'm in the business of building empires, but I didn't start out with one. Not even close. At the beginning, I was stuffed into a cubicle at a crummy job I hated. It's interesting how the time between then and now, the hard times, always gets compressed.

In hindsight, *of course* all the struggles were worth it—but that's only with the perspective of what I know now. Because today, after coaching hundreds of my students into their own $10,000-per-month ecommerce businesses, I know that anyone can do this. Seriously.

Don't believe me? Then it's my hope that by the end of this book, I will have changed your mind. Because to make money at this—and I'm talking about the kind of income that can empower you to take back control of your life—you only need a few things. And I'm going to tell you exactly what they are and specifically what steps you must take to acquire them.

To create an Ecommerce Empire, the kind that can earn you $10,000+ a month, you don't need a college education. Just ask the high schooler in my course who is making $1,000 a week with this method.

You don't need sophisticated skills in data analysis or marketing. I have a degree in computer science, after all.

You don't need a rich benefactor or investors to bankroll product design or to buy you a huge warehouse to store it all. I can get you started with less than $500, and none of my students have packages stored in their living rooms.

But even though you have the tools to be successful, that doesn't necessarily mean you will be. According to Forbes, 543,000 new businesses are started each month. But about 80% of those crash and burn their first year.

Why are so many of these start-ups failing? Are the odds really this stacked against you?

Here's the deal: Having an online storefront and expecting sales to magically appear is no longer enough. Throwing together a business through Amazon or Etsy is unlikely to be successful. You might make a little money or break even, but you'll probably lose some with every transaction. Yet most folks get started on one of these platforms. No wonder so many people think it's impossible to make money in ecommerce.

But that's not going to be you, because I'm going to give you the tools to get up and running and profitable within a month. How? Control.

As a new business owner, you must be in control of everything, from the moment a potential customer lands on your site to the times they come back to it again and again. You are going to craft what your prospect sees, choose where they navigate to, and curate their entire experience.

You aren't going to create a trend or a fad; you're going to build a future-proof business.

I was an 18-year-old freshman when I learned about making money online through affiliate marketing. Back then, I was your typical young adult. I had no clue what I wanted to do with my life. I was a total introvert and spent most of my time playing World of Warcraft in my dorm room. I majored in computer science because I figured computers weren't going anywhere, and that way I could play video games all the time.

I wasn't a pillar of maturity back then. And I definitely wasn't ready to build a business. I think I just sort of assumed, maybe by default, that I'd somehow get a good job working for some IT company that would pay me a decent wage.

And that's funny, because my parents were entrepreneurs. Not really by choice, but by necessity. They had immigrated to the US from Poland when they were 16 and 17. They didn't speak any English. Not a word. And when you don't speak English in America, you can't always depend on someone to give you a job. They had to make it happen for themselves.

And they did find success in a few different ventures, including real estate. All in all, my parents were pretty shrewd entrepreneurs. And while they instilled that kind of work ethic in their kids, they never really wanted us to take on that kind of risk.

Of course, as a quiet kid playing video games in my room, I wasn't ready then. But ready or not, that first year of school is when I met my first mentor.

Mo was also my best friend, an 18-year-old college roommate who was just as immature as me. We spent most of our free time hanging out in our dorm, eating chicken fingers and fries from the dining hall, playing PlayStation, and sometimes going to class. We definitely weren't cultivating a strong sense of entrepreneurialism...or at least I didn't think so.

But one day I came back from a database architectures class to find Mo jumping around and yelling, "I just made a hundred bucks!"

"What? Did you get a job or something?"

He laughed. "No, I made a commission!"

I was completely dumbfounded. "For doing what exactly? Break it down for me."

"You know when you go to a car dealership to buy a car?"

"You know I don't have a car."

"Fine, but you know how *some* people go to a dealership to buy a car? The people on the sales floor make money every time they sell one. And I'm basically that salesperson, but online. I sold somebody's product online, and I made a hundred bucks in commission."

I was so confused. I couldn't believe that anyone—especially my roommate—could make money like this. I asked Mo every question I could think of. Do you need a website? Do you need sales training? How do you find the products? Who pays you and how? How is this even possible?!

"Chill, bro."

Mo promised to show me everything...but first I had to commit to this new career. So I dedicated myself with the kind of obsessiveness that only an introverted WoW-creating, video game-playing nerd can. I was all in.

We read books. We visited online forums. We took courses. I remember leaving my study group in the library to hop on the phone with an affiliate marketer I'd paid to teach me how to do this stuff. Mo and I pursued online marketing to the extent that we effectively received two degrees: an official one in computer science and an unofficial one in making money online.

And it actually paid off! I think we made about $200 to $300 a week. Not bad for a couple of college kids. I remember getting my biggest check of $800 from some company that paid me using a money market account. I didn't have a bank account, so I had to send it to my mom so she could cash it for me. You can imagine how shocked my Polish mother was when I asked her to cash some strange-looking check. She called and said, "Pete, what are you doing? Is this check even real?" (Even I was a little surprised when it cleared.)

Although I made a little cash back then, I wasn't making enough for a full-time career. So I went to (some of) my classes, graduated, and tried to pursue the American Dream with a job that I…

absolutely…

completely…

and totally HATED.

Every minute of every day was agony. Picture the kind of offices that are depicted in comedies. The ones in huge buildings where you could accidentally get off on the wrong floor, walk to where your desk should be, and wonder why you're suddenly looking at a photo of some other guy's family. We were all crammed into tiny cubicles. The air was filled with that awkward quietness of 30 people typing miserably. Maybe some boring chat coming from the water cooler. None of us really cared about what we were doing there. We were complacent. It got to the point where a morning cup of coffee or afternoon doughnut was the biggest highlight of my day.

I was, in a word, miserable.

I don't mean to knock anyone who's working a nine-to-five or traditional job. Tons of satisfied people are employed by great companies that do important work and motivate their workforce. I was just the wrong guy for that particular role.

Have you ever experienced one of those surreal moments where you sit back, look at where you are, and think, *This just isn't me?* Obviously it IS you, but it's like you're an actor who was just placed in the wrong role, and you're wondering why the director hasn't figured it out yet.

One day, I was sitting in the break room, going through the motions of yet another day, watching one my coworkers shuffle out for a smoke break. My girlfriend and I (she was actually my first girlfriend) had broken up earlier that year. All my friends from college were living somewhere else, doing something else. Mo had returned to his hometown. And here I was, in a cubicle that faced away from the windows at a company I would probably stay with until I retired, on track for a legacy as "that one tech support guy."

And I wondered, *What is the point of all this?*

I tried to think back to the last time I was happy and realized it was when I was hanging out in my dorm room, hustling affiliate marketing style, making a couple hundred bucks a week. I had loved so many things about marketing. I loved learning new skills and problem solving. I loved the freedom of it all, that I could fail or succeed based on my own merit. And I had learned just as much, if not more, in this youthful pursuit of my "second degree" in marketing.

Would I really stay in this crummy job and effectively toss out all that knowledge and experience? Of course, a huge part of me was hesitant. It felt so irresponsible, like chasing a pipe dream.

Could I really make money online full-time as an adult?

Despite the risk and uncertainty, that idea took hold. Over the next few months, I started building a side hustle after work and on the weekends. But this wouldn't be some teenager's attempt to make a little money online.

I wanted to build something systematic, profitable, and scalable. To create a business out of nothing in the way my parents had. If they could build something great without any resources whatsoever, I could do the same.

But unlike affiliate marketing, I wouldn't make *other* people money by promoting their products. And I wouldn't allow myself to be limited by whatever commission they doled out. Instead, I'd control the product, and therefore the profits.

I was going to build an Ecommerce Empire.

When I started my first ecommerce business, I had very little money. So I had to figure out how to spend my life savings, about $5,000, very wisely. I invested all of it into Amazon. Fulfillment by Amazon (FBA) is a service available to people who sell items on that site. With FBA, you store your products in Amazon's fulfillment centers, and they pack, ship, and provide customer service. The program allows you to source inexpensive products from China, have them sent to an FBA warehouse, and then Amazon sells them for you.

I didn't have to work too hard to find products. I didn't have to arrange storage. I didn't have to store product in my garage, ship boxes, deal with returns, or handle money. While I was waiting for my first order, I was so excited I could barely sleep.

I call the year when I got into the program the "Wild West of FBA." During that time, just about anyone could sell anything through the program and absolutely crush it. The main reason was that there simply wasn't much competition—Amazon was the only retailer with this type of program, and few people were taking advantage of it. My business was no exception.

Things happened fast. By the end of the first year, my business did $80,000 per month in sales.

I thought I had everything figured out. I was sourcing products and marketing them successfully. I was a business owner. And not just any owner—one who was making a profit.

There was just one problem: I was still working full-time.

I bet you're thinking, *Pete! If you did $80,000 a month in sales, why didn't you quit your job?!*

That's a good question, and one that I was learning the answer to.

Even though I was doing a high volume of sales, I wasn't actually making much in terms of profit. At least not enough to leave my job. In fact, most of my capital was tied up in inventory. Every time I turned a profit, I'd reinvest in more product. And because Amazon was taking a cut on top of that, I wasn't able to grow my business AND take an income. I was stuck.

So as I ate lunch in my tiny cubicle, I would watch as tens of thousands of dollars were deposited into my account…and just as quickly withdrawn to pay for more inventory.

Six months later, my life spiraled out of control.

I was driving to work, feeling pretty good. Sure, I still had to work 40 hours a week doing something I hated, but I could see a path forward. Eventually, with the help of FBA, I'd be able to quit my job.

But then my phone dinged. Stuck in traffic, I opened my screen to find an email from Amazon: "Your listing has been suppressed."

I set my phone down, planning to look into it during my first break.

Then I heard another ding. And then another. And another. And another.

Your listing has been suppressed.
Your listing has been suppressed.
Your listing has been suppressed.
Your listing has been suppressed.

Within 10 minutes, all five of my products had been removed from Amazon.

I broke into a shivering, cold sweat. When traffic started to move again, I sped to my workplace, dove into the elevator, agonized as I waited for it to climb to the eighteenth floor, raced to my cubicle, and turned on my computer without breathing a word to anyone. I'm not sure I even breathed at all.

By the time I pulled up my Amazon account, my products and I had been banned from the site.

That same day, I learned from another Amazon email that it was due to false IP claims made against the business. What the hell?

A competitor claimed that my company had infringed on some of their patents. Although this wasn't true (I was selling everyday products), Amazon wasn't about to get caught in a legal battle between sellers. So they removed my products from the platform, insisting that all parties had to resolve the issues independently.

It took a year to get that account back. But the damage had already been done.

I had nothing. Nothing but an empty investment account and a dead-end job. Nothing except for all the promises I had made that—an hour ago—I had thought I could actually keep.

Promises to my mom to help her retire early.

Promises to the rest of the world that I'd prove this was possible.

Promises that an immigrant kid could realize his American Dream.

Promises to myself that I'd leave my job soon.

I was left with $40,000 of product I couldn't sell and a journal filled with goals that now seemed impossible.

Within 10 minutes, my business had been tanked. I had no revenue and no email addresses. I couldn't even follow up with my customers to explain what had happened. And that's when I learned a very painful lesson, one that I desperately want to save you from learning the hard way.

You see, no one (except for me and my mom) cared that my business was destroyed. My customers didn't notice I was gone. They just bought from my competitors instead. Amazon had plenty of other marketers lining up to take my place.

I had set out to build a business that would allow me more control and autonomy than I had through affiliate marketing. I wanted to have my own customers and to control my profits. Yet these had all been Amazon's customers, not mine.

Amazon wasn't helping me build MY business…I was helping them build theirs.

Remember this: Amazon, Shopify, Etsy, eBay, and any other platforms like them don't care about you. It didn't care about me. It didn't care about my friends who had built a million-dollar-a-month business on Amazon only to lose it all and return to their full-time jobs.

I don't want that for you. I won't let it happen.

If you are selling on one of these platforms, or if you're considering it, I hope you'll read to the end of this book. Because it's one thing to show you what can happen if you go down that path, but it's entirely another to prove to you that **there is a different option out there—a better one**.

I want you to take all the information in this book so you can skip over the part where you lose your life savings and instead fast-forward to the point where you start making a living for yourself.

I want to teach you how to build a profitable business that YOU control.

I want you to be able to tell your friends and family that you are building an Ecommerce Empire.

After the FBA incident, I had to start from zero…again. Really, I was starting off worse than before. My life savings were gone. I had started a new relationship and it wasn't going so well. I was still showing up to my terrible job. To be honest, this was a dark period of my life. I couldn't even fathom starting another business.

So many entrepreneurs have hit that place. Maybe you've been there before. But you just get into this loop. You eat, work, sleep, repeat. Resigned to defeat.

And if you've been there, or even if you're in it now, I'm going to help you get out of it. Because while having a business or even just a little side hustle in ecommerce might feel out of reach now, I know that it isn't. Maybe you tried and got burned, but you picked this book up because some part of you knows that it's still possible.

Or you might be at the beginning of your journey and I've just terrified you. If you are, you need to know that you will inevitably encounter unforeseen problems, maybe even hardships, that you can't possibly predict. I have no interest in lying to you. This business is not easy.

But that doesn't mean you shouldn't go for it.

I'm here to be your guide. Yes, you'll make mistakes, but I'm going to ensure that you don't make any big ones. More importantly, I want to help you cultivate the mindset you'll need to overcome all the roadblocks you will face.

If you have tried and failed in the past, I want to give you the confidence to try again.

I know you can do this. You just didn't have all the information and tools the first time around. But with the information in this book and a failure or two under your belt, you'll come back stronger than before.

This is a compilation of everything I've learned over 10 years of building up a successful ecommerce business and helping my students create more than 1,000 funnels. And all of my wins and losses have culminated in **a method that is low-risk and low-cost.**

Everything I am about to share with you I learned from doing the opposite. My FBA business was extremely high-cost and enormously high-risk. So I'm going to teach you how to create a business with…

- A small initial investment (less than $500)
- Very little risk

Plus you aren't going to struggle to source an awesome product. And you aren't going to warehouse it in your garage or drop off packages at UPS five times a day.

And the best part?

You are going to build a business that is not only profitable but also enjoyable.

You are going to build an empire.

It doesn't matter whether you make a million dollars with your business (although I hope I can convince you it's possible). It doesn't matter whether you quit your job like I did. Plenty of successful business owners go to a nine-to-five they love, and work on their ecommerce business on the side because it's something they enjoy doing.

This book isn't about you molding a business that looks exactly like mine.

You are going to create your empire, whatever that means to you.

But I'm not just here to show you the specific actions you should take to build your business. By the end of this book, you will have your own personalized funnel based on the same structure that has earned my clients $10K a month or more.

Creating your funnel is going to be one of the most critical elements of your success. But giving you all the steps without preparing you for the hurdles is like giving you a list of ingredients without a recipe.

Sure you must understand each component (and you will), but you also need the instruction manual. At the end of this book, a pre-built funnel is waiting for you. However, the rest of these pages are the manual. Without reading this first, you will have a hard time operating the equipment.

For that reason, I highly encourage you to read from start to finish and consider the strategies I'm sharing. Take the time to complete the Empire Builder Exercises in each chapter. They are intended to act as a blueprint for your future business. That way, I can keep my promise to you…

By the end of this book, you will be well on your way to building an Ecommerce Empire.

And how are you going to build that empire? This is my roadmap to seven figures—$1 million!

Reaching a million in sales will be a monumental milestone for you. And right now, it might seem so far out of reach that it's impossible. But it IS possible, and here's how you're going to do it.

Over the course of this book, I'm going to teach you how to build an Ecommerce Empire built on customized funnels to drive traffic that YOU control.

I've dedicated a full chapter to the nuts and bolts of a funnel, but for now just think of it as a series of pages that lead traffic (online buyers) to a sale, a more profitable way to sell products online.

I also plan to change the way you think about money. When I say seven figures, you might feel nervous. So let's break it down.

You're going to build each of your funnels around a different ecommerce product. Let's say you do 25 sales a day for each funnel. (Yes, I am going to teach you how to get those sales. For now, just trust me that you'll have them.)

Each of those sales is going to have an average cart value of $30. (Yep, I'm going to teach you how to get the right cart value too. Don't worry—you ARE going to hit this number!)

In the example below, each funnel represents a different product. You'll learn how to choose the right product for you. In this example, I use various body-building supplements.

#1. PRE-WORKOUT
25 SALES PER DAY X $30 AVERAGE CART = $750

#2. WHEY PROTEIN POWDER
25 SALES PER DAY X $30 AVERAGE CART = $750

#3. RECOVERY SHAKE
25 SALES PER DAY X $30 AVERAGE CART = $750

#4. MULTIVITAMIN
25 SALES PER DAY X $30 AVERAGE CART = $750

Now let's see how much you're doing in sales each day.

$$750 \times 4 = \$3,000$$

And how many sales are you doing a year?

$$\$3,000 \times 365 = \$1,095,000$$

That's over a million in sales a year, just from four products! Even after you subtract the cost of buying product, that is some serious net profit.

My goal is not to teach you how to build a business that is exactly like mine. Today, my Ecommerce Empire nets millions of dollars each year and employs more than 30 people. But that might not be what you want.

Maybe you love your current job and you just want to supplement your income a bit. And you know what? That's absolutely fine. This isn't about what I want for you, it's about what YOU want for you.

That being said, I'm going to help you break down barriers around what you think you can achieve, because in my experience, the biggest obstacle most people face is their own self-imposed limitations. But unlike how it happened for me, it's not going to take you a decade to figure out how to do it.

You're holding the blueprint to success in your hands.

Your empire starts now.

CHAPTER 1

THE EMPIRE BUILDER'S MINDSET

Now that you know my story—how I went from $0 to $80,000 a month and back to $0 again, then rebuilt my online business to seven figures—you have a little insight into what I'm going to say next.

Everything else I tell you in this book—like how to choose a product, create an offer, and use the built-for-you funnel you'll get at the end—that's all the easy stuff. Once you understand how each piece fits together, you'll have all the tools to build your empire. But those will be completely useless without the right mindset.

I promised that if you're feeling defeated or daunted by ecommerce, I'd help you overcome that. And I can do that because I've had to do so myself. After I lost everything in the FBA business, I was so depressed that I didn't even notice when I started to lose track of the most significant things in my life, like my goals and hopes for the future. And over the next two years, I grew a chip on my shoulder.

I blamed Amazon.

I blamed that competitor who reported me.

I blamed bad luck.

I blamed everyone and everything…

Except for myself.

One Saturday morning—I'm not sure why—I walked over to my bookshelf and picked up a book I had bought two years prior, while in college. It was *The Slight Edge* by Jeff Olsen, the first book I ever read on entrepreneurship. It prompted the reader to write their goals right inside the book, and there staring back at me were my goals from that time.

One in particular stood out. By the age of 25, I wanted to make $20,000 a month. (Yeah, I was a pretty ambitious teenager.) Yet here I was at 24, making only $3,500 a month. Which could have been all right, if I hadn't been so miserable.

Where was the guy who believed he could achieve that goal? What happened to him? At that moment, I didn't resemble the person my 18-year-old self had believed I could be. I was nothing like him.

It's so easy to be passionate about something when things are going well, isn't it? When you're making money or in a great relationship or at a job you like. It's effortless to set big goals, stay up late, and work on Saturdays. When it's already good, it's natural to want to make it even better.

Back in college, I had all these dreams and expectations for myself. And I really thought I could achieve them, because why not? If I was making a couple hundred bucks a week as a college student, why wouldn't I expect myself to be rich as an adult?

But when things went south, my passion disappeared. I couldn't handle it, so I quit.

Holding that book in my hands, I imagined what my life might look like if I stayed with the company. Up every day at eight, half an hour commute, in my cubicle by nine. Doughnuts and coffee. And I knew that I'd eventually grow bitter and resentful. Then 30 years later, I'd retire as a cranky, old tech support guy.

You see, during those early days in my online business, I had the tools to make money online, but I didn't have the mindset I needed. I could manage being a business owner during the good times, when I was doing tens of thousands of dollars in sales each month. Who couldn't? But when the bad times came, I just wasn't ready.

Thinking about that disconnect between the person my 18-year-old self had imagined and the person I had become, I had an epiphany.

I wanted to start my own business.

I wanted to be rich.

I wanted to travel the world and buy nice things and help my mom retire early.

I wanted all those things, but I didn't *act* like I did. I did not make the choices or take the actions that someone who could achieve those goals would.

So I decided I would try again.

But this time, I wasn't going to quit the first time I stumbled.

THE FORCE HOLDING YOU BACK

The most amazing part about being an entrepreneur is the moments when you are just blowing past your goals. You're under budget and zooming ahead of what you thought you could make.

Let me tell you, it's an incredible feeling when you realize you're on track to make more than you ever made at your desk job. (Imagine what it's going to be like to double it!) All these successes are happening around you, while you have the freedom and flexibility to design your life however you want.

I get up early every day because I honestly love what I do, and I can't wait to get started each morning. But if I wanted, I could sleep in until 9 a.m., take a couple months off during the year, and still retire early. Having that kind of control over your work and life is fantastic.

But those highs are always tempered by moments when you get so low you question your own sanity. Times when you get home late from work and you still have to muster the energy to build your business. Learning to say no to friends on the weekends. Saving every dollar to reinvest in yourself and your business.

And if you're just dipping your toes into being your own boss, that all might sound melodramatic. But if you've tried—and failed—you know exactly what I'm talking about.

I'm going to show you how to create a business that will allow you to make whatever kind of life for yourself that you want. But it will not come easily and it won't be without some risk. I'm asking you to bet on yourself.

I can't predict every possible obstacle you will face, but what I do know with certainty is that you will have *something* to overcome.

And if you aren't prepared for that inevitability, you'll be set up to fail.

And you are not going to fail, because YOU are going to cultivate the mindset of an Empire Builder. To do that, you must determine the force that is holding you back.

Now I'm about to say something pretty harsh, but stick with me, because once you accept these hard truths, you'll be free. Uninhibited to completely dedicate yourself to your goal.

Ready? Here it is.

Nothing is guaranteed.
No one owes you anything.
And no one truly cares about what you want.

There is a reason some people get what they want and others don't. Why some achieve seemingly amazing things and others don't. A lot of people, and maybe this sounds like some people in your life now, all they do is complain.

They whine about their awful jobs and their crappy salaries and their mean bosses. They criticize their friends or grumble about their relationships. Yet they do nothing to change their circumstances. Not too long ago, I was that guy—blaming everyone but myself for my own predicament.

From this day forward, you are going to bet on yourself. You are going to take personal responsibility for your own goals. And you are going to create the life you want for yourself and your family.

As I mentioned in my story, there was a major difference between the person I wanted to become and the person I was. I suspect you might feel that way too. Think about who you are now, in this moment. Consider your mindset and personality, but also your routines and habits.

What time do you wake up in the morning?

How do you take control over your time? Or do you often waste it?

How many hours each day or week do you allocate to achieving your goals, strengthening your relationships, or learning a new skill?

Now compare the person you are now to the person you will need to become to achieve your goals.

Current You, let me introduce you to New You. Here a few qualities you now have.

You don't hope or expect that someone else will make you wealthy.

I've met a lot of people who hope that success and money will fall into their laps, as if they could just stumble upon fortune. And maybe some do, but if one thing is true of capitalism, it's that no one is just going to *let* you become wealthy.

You don't rely on an employer for your financial freedom. You have accepted that no one else is responsible for how much money you make. You don't hope and pray that something will work itself out. Instead you have a clear vision, and you will execute it.

You surround yourself with people who have similar goals.

You know that if you want to succeed, you must surround yourself with people with like mindsets. Not everyone will share your vision, and not everyone will want you to succeed. That can be a tough pill to swallow, but for a few people in your life, your ambition will remind them of how little they've accomplished. So they will want to tear you down.

But the New You understands this, so you are careful about who you confide in. And you hang out with people who want you to succeed, who think like you do, and who want to learn and develop right along with you.

You are in control.

You know that if you aren't making the money you want to, that is your fault. You accept that your past choices, for better or worse, have brought you to where you are today. And if you don't like how that looks, you don't accept defeat. Because you know that YOU have the power to change your circumstances.

You are in charge of how you spend your time. You realize that it is the most valuable resource you have, so you guard it carefully. And you know that the only force holding you back is you.

Are you ready to become this person? If you are willing to make a change, you need to do what others don't to achieve what others won't. Lots of people set goals—big, impressive, meaningful ones. But then a month later, they've quit.

That's not you. You are going to be strict with yourself because you know that every choice you make has a direct correlation to your success or failure.

If you choose to sleep in today, it will affect your life.

If you decide to quit working early, it will affect your life.

Listen, there will always be something demanding your attention. Your cell phone. Netflix. Your cat. Your neighbors, friends, or family.

Sometimes you must turn your phone off and put it in a drawer, turn off the TV, and lock your pets in the next room.

Sometimes you'll even have to say no to people you love.

But other times you'll allow yourself to be distracted because you've decided that something is worth your time and because it's important to you. You'll spend a night with your friends or take an early Friday to have dinner with your partner.

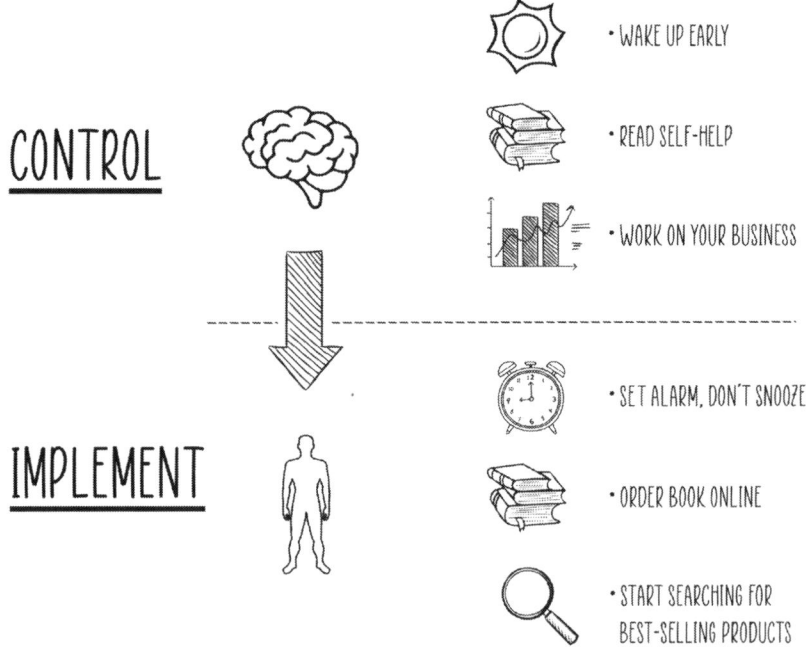

The difference is that it's a choice you make because you are in control of your time.

> **EMPIRE BUILDER EXERCISE**
>
> Now that I've gotten you to start thinking about the New You, take some time to consider your legacy.
>
> How do you wish to be remembered?
>
> What will you leave to your children or nieces and nephews?
>
> In what specific ways will you impact the world?
>
> How will you achieve it?
>
> Describe your ideal legacy below.

FEEDBACK LOOPS AND RESISTANCE

Many businesses fail. Actually, *most* businesses fail. And it's not because the start-up owner is lazy. Most entrepreneurs put tons of effort into their businesses. But when they hit their first obstacle, they question their business model or their own capabilities, and they quit.

That's what I did the first time around.

Why do so many of us give up when we hit a wall? There are two reasons: resistance and the absence of feedback.

Resistance

Resistance ties into the previous section on being uncomfortable. When someone feels resistance, they want to get back to a situation that is comfortable and familiar. It's wanting to turn the hot water back on at the end of your shower, hitting the snooze button because you'd rather stay in bed, and staying in that nine-to-five job because you've been doing it for so long.

If you took a random person out of their cubicle and asked them to build their own business from the ground up, most likely they wouldn't be able to do it. Not because they don't have the experience or knowledge, but because they are afraid.

You will get to a point where you can quit your job because your ecommerce business can support you. When that happens, you will face resistance. Most people are scared to bet on themselves. You won't be.

Because you will understand that growth and comfort do not go hand-in-hand. If you are always comfortable, you cannot grow. And if you are always growing, you are not going to be comfortable. Don't worry—eventually, you'll get comfortable being uncomfortable.

Feedback Loops

You are going to create an Empire Builder feedback loop by considering both your failures and your successes as data points. You will distance yourself from any emotional connection with these events.

Your failures will no longer be personal.

They don't mean that YOU are a failure, but simply that a choice you made did not turn out the way you expected. It doesn't matter whether you have a great sales day or a bad one. It is only one data point, and you will adjust as you need to.

The New You will take some kind of action, like creating a new ad or finding a unique product. You'll measure or quantify the results of that action, analyze them, then make corrections and improvements. Here's what your new feedback loops will look like:

1. Take action.
2. Measure.
3. Analyze.
4. Adjust.
5. Repeat.

The key to learning from your failures is to treat each one as simply a data point. You no longer have any emotional ties if the results aren't in your favor. You are personally removed from the experience, like a scientist recording observations and adjusting the experiment accordingly. Even when you get the desired results, you are still going to take this approach. Nothing is ever perfect.

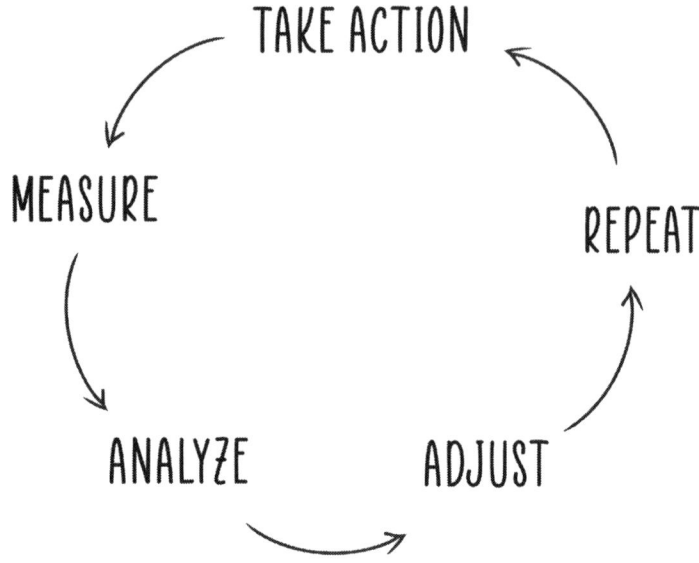

MASTER AND PUPPET

I'm going to bet that you've been living every day as if your body and mind are one thing. But I want you to start thinking about them as two separate entities. And each of them needs exercise.

Just like there are many ways you can exercise your muscles, there are numerous methods you can use to train your mind, like meditation, daily reading, and building better habits.

But before you can do that, you have to acknowledge the sometimes difficult relationship that most of us have with our minds and bodies. So often there is a disconnect when your mind wants one thing and your body wants another.

Think about what it's like trying to wake up early. Your mind wants to, but your body says no. There are so many examples to choose from. Eating healthy, working out, going to bed early. How about when your friends ask you to go out for drinks on Friday night and your mind says, *No, don't do that! You're going to waste your entire Saturday!* Yet there you are, having a few too many beers and being hung over the next day.

So often what's best for us—what we *want*—doesn't line up with what we actually *do*.

Have you ever run a marathon? A strange thing happens when some people see the finish line. Despite having run fine for the entire race, once the runner sees that tape, they collapse before crossing. Their minds know they only have a bit longer to go, but their bodies just give up.

I think about the disconnect between body and mind as a master and puppet. I'm willing to bet that until this day, your body has pulled the strings of your mind.

Consider this the day that changes. Visualize your mind as the puppet master of your body.

Control is everything. I don't want you to be under the power of anything, not even your own limitations. For your mind to become the puppeteer of your body, you'll need to train it. One of the best ways to do that is to do activities that take you out of your usual routine.

You need to get comfortable being uncomfortable.

Here are some daily challenges you can use to train your brain this week, starting tomorrow.

- **DAY ONE: Wake up an hour earlier than you normally would.**
  You will probably want to hit snooze. Don't do it! As soon as your alarm goes off, your mind is now in control. Tell your body to get out of bed.

- **DAY TWO: Take a cold shower.**
  This is one of my favorite exercises. Before you hop out of the shower, turn the water to freezing cold. Stand in the cold water and count to 10. When you do this (especially after a workout), you strengthen the power of your mind over your body. That cold shower might be the hardest thing you do that day, but I promise you will feel accomplished.

- **DAY THREE: Say no to something.**
  Maybe it's evening drinks or a movie with your friends. You need to maintain those relationships, but you also have to be in control of how you spend your time. Instead of grabbing drinks (which will ruin your weekend), spend your Friday night reading this book. Try limiting your nights out with friends to one or two times a month, and spend those hours gained by strengthening your business (and your resolve). Use this newfound time to focus on your Ecommerce Empire.

- **DAY FOUR: Add five minutes to your daily workout.**
  (Or try a 10-minute workout if you don't already.) Exercise is not only critical to understanding the master and puppet concept, it's also crucial to your overall well-being.

- **DAY FIVE: Eat food that you normally wouldn't choose.**
  Variation is critical. If you usually order a steak, try the weirdest vegetarian meal on the menu. Go to a different restaurant. Cook a healthy recipe. Change up your diet to help your body understand that even though it wants that juicy steak, the mind is always in charge.

- **DAYS SIX AND SEVEN: Stack a new challenge with an old habit.**
  Stacking is a common practice in habit creation where you pair a new habit with an old one as a way of more easily changing behavior. For example, if adding an extra 10 minutes to your workout was especially helpful to you, try to make that challenge part of your routine by linking that behavior with something you already do, like drinking coffee or eating lunch.

  Habit stacking is a powerful tool to adopt new, and better, routines. If this exercise has been helpful to you, brainstorm other ways you can use stacking to improve yourself. For example, if you always have a cup of coffee first thing in the morning, try to stack that habit with one that will improve your business (or your life), like journaling your goals or coming up with new product ideas.

Are you ready to try it yourself? In the next Empire Builders Exercise, you'll write down your daily personal goals for this week.

If you make up your own challenges instead of using the ones I mentioned, consider the role that variation plays in the master and puppet concept. It can be helpful to imagine that within everyone, there are various versions of them, kind of like pieces to a puzzle.

The successful version has different habits, tastes, and routines than the social version or the indulgent one, for example. By constantly testing and trying new things, you can tap into the version of you that is capable of meeting your goals.

EMPIRE BUILDER EXERCISE

Fill out the table below with your daily challenges.

DAY ONE

DAY TWO

DAY THREE

DAY FOUR

DAY FIVE

DAY SIX

DAY SEVEN

Also, repeat this affirmation to yourself daily:

"I am going to become comfortable with being uncomfortable."

That's an Empire Builder's mindset.

This has been a crash course in the kind of mindset you'll need to adopt to meet the goals you'll outline in the very last chapter. I hope you continue to work on mindset throughout your entrepreneurial journey, as there is always something you can do to move your business forward and improve your life in general.

And never forget, YOU are the force holding you back. At least you were. But now you've met the New You, the one who…

- Doesn't hope or expect someone else to make you wealthy.
- Surrounds yourself with people who have similar goals.
- Knows YOU are in control.

And you understand that you have to become mentally strong, put yourself in uncomfortable situations, and take control over your body. Remember, from this day forward, your MIND is in control.

Why is that essential in ecommerce? Because you will use your newfound control to view your successes and failures dispassionately, through the lens of data. You will no longer be emotionally connected to your business; instead, you will conduct an experiment where you pull certain levers and measure the outcome.

And at times, you will have to make hard choices because you're on the cusp of building something great. If you want a side hustle, this could be the difference between retiring early or working into your seventies. If you want to do a million in sales a year, you can leave something that will last generations.

I know I'm being a bit tough on you, but that's because by choosing to read this book, you're already so much further than most people. And I can't have you passing out like those runners who never make it to the finish line. No, you are going all the way.

And remember…you won't fail if you never quit.

That's an Empire Builder's mindset.

Next we're going to start building that empire. The first step is to choose the right niche.

CHAPTER 2

FIND THE RIGHT NICHE

After deciding to rebuild my business as a result of losing everything on Amazon, I learned how to choose a market and niche the hard way. I built hundreds of different funnels for hundreds of random products. I sold flag football sets, agility cones and ladders, gavels, stadium cushion seats, and coin-collecting sleeves and protectors. I even sold those little stickers of moms, dads, kids, and pets that you put on car windows.

Most of these products checked all the boxes in terms of profitability. They were easy to source, ship, and upsell. Other people were making money selling them, and they were in high demand. On paper, they made sense.

So why didn't I make any money?

In hindsight, all these products were doomed to underperform from the beginning. It's not that they were bad products, it's just that I didn't really care about stickers.

And that's when I realized something: I had to find a product that I would enjoy selling so much that I wouldn't care if it was successful or not, because I'd have such a great time building the funnel and interacting with my customers. I asked myself, "What will I love five years from now?" I wanted to understand what kind of products I could sell for the rest of my life and not get bored by them.

I love fishing. When I was growing up, my parents didn't have a lot of money. They couldn't afford for me to join any of the sports teams at my high school or anything like that. So they were always trying to figure out inexpensive and fun activities we could do together. My dad's ultimate solution was fishing.

We used to go up to the Pocono mountains in Pennsylvania on the weekends. Every time, my dad would rent the cheapest motel in the area…and still negotiate a lower price. We would wake up super early, around 5 a.m., just so we could be the first on the lake. We would rent this beat-up old boat that didn't even have a motor (just oars) for like $20 a day, while other people on the lake blew past us in their gas-powered top-of-the-line fishing boats. But it didn't matter to me—I loved every second of it.

So I built a business around something I knew a lot about and genuinely loved doing. And guess what? That's when I realized the power of immersing yourself in a business you genuinely care about.

UNDERSTANDING NICHES AND MARKETS

To create your Ecommerce Empire, you need to start your business in a market that you care about. You are going to spend a ton of time totally immersed in this space, so do yourself a favor and choose something you actually enjoy.

I realize that you might be thinking, *I don't care what I sell, I just need it to be profitable.* But once that money starts flowing, you won't feel that way anymore. I know this because it happened to me. And it still happens to clients who ignore my advice.

I've seen so many people build up extremely profitable businesses, only to burn out after six months or a year. And wasting all that time spent researching, sourcing, and testing the products, building the funnels, and drawing in traffic.

But you aren't going to squander your time, because you will have a head start—you're going to choose the right niche in the right market.

A **market** is a broad category or industry. I have identified eight markets that encompass nearly the entire world of ecommerce. If you already have a product in mind, chances are it falls under one of those categories.

- Beauty
- Dating and Relationships
- Fitness
- Health
- Hobbies
- Pets
- Self-Improvement
- Weight loss

Within the markets, there are smaller categories called **niches**.

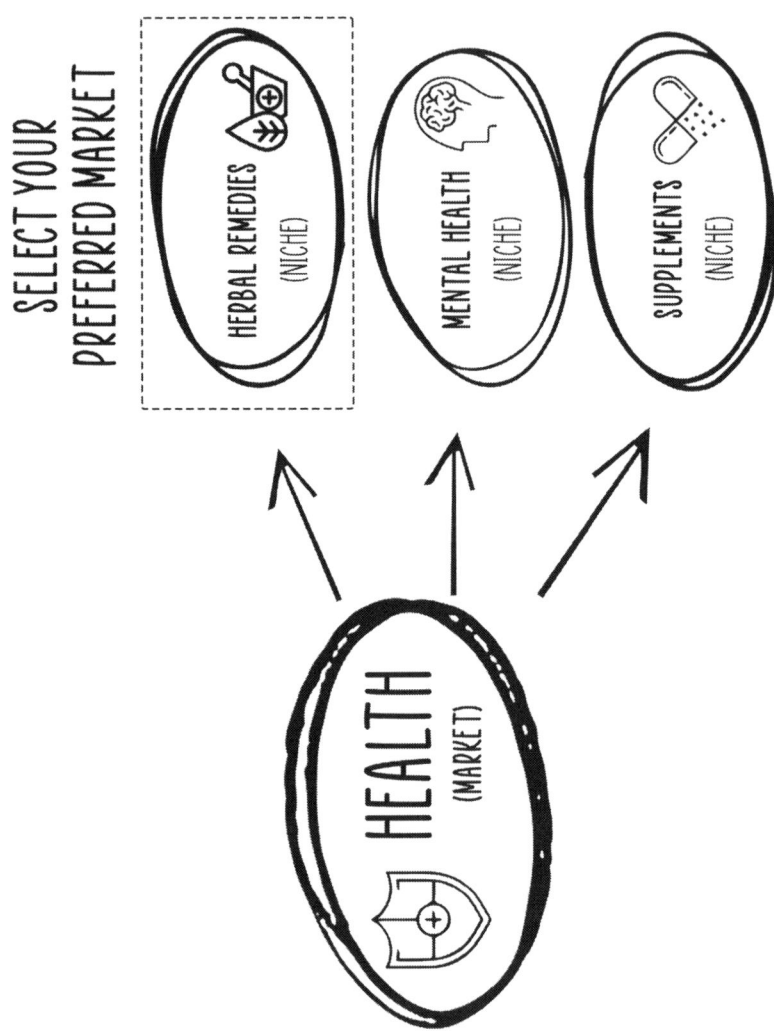

Following are a few more examples.

MARKETS	NICHES
BEAUTY	AGING, CLOTHING, MAKEUP
DATING AND RELATIONSHIPS	LOVE AND ROMANCE, MARRIAGE COUNSELING, ONLINE DATING
FITNESS	RUNNING, WEIGHT TRAINING, WORKOUT ROUTINES
HEALTH	HERBAL REMEDIES, MENTAL HEALTH, SUPPLEMENTS
HOBBIES	GAMING, OUTDOOR RECREATION, SPORTS
PETS	CHOOSING PETS, EDUCATION AND RESEARCH, TRAINING PETS
SELF-IMPROVEMENT	GOAL SETTING, HABITS, MINDSET
WEIGHT LOSS	DIET PLANS, PROGRAMS DEFINED BY AGE, WEIGHT, OR GENDER, TARGETED WEIGHT-LOSS EXERCISES

You don't want to get into an entire market. It's way too broad. In terms of selecting a niche, if you came to me and said, "Pete, I'm going into fitness!" I'd say, "No way!" There is still such a huge variation within markets.

Consider how many types of people are within the fitness market. You have runners, mountain climbers, pole vaulters, cross-fitters, and bikers. I'm sure you can list at least 20 more categories that belong in fitness off the top of your head.

If you said, "Pete, I'm going into running!" I'd still say, "That's too broad as well!" Within a group of runners, you could

EMPIRE BUILDER EXERCISE

Select one market that interests you from the previous table.

Brainstorm 10 niches within it that you can picture yourself working in five years from now.

What will you still enjoy doing?

You don't have to get it 100% right here. This is just a chance for you to explore some options. I'll help you zone in more as we go.

MARKET:

POSSIBLE NICHES IN MY MARKET

1.
2.
3.
4.
5.
6.
7.
8.
9.
10.

have trail runners, marathoners, ultra-marathoners, ultra-marathoner trail-runners, sprinters, cross-country racers, and casual runners who speed walk around the block. And within those groups, each can still be divided by age or gender. What about female ultra-marathoner trail runners? Or how about folks over the age of 60 who have never run a day in their life but would like to start?

This is the difference between a niche and a **subniche**—a laser-targeted, super-specific category within a market. Throughout the rest of the book, when I say "niche," I'm really talking about a subniche. Here are a few more examples to illustrate the difference.

MARKET	HEALTH
NICHES	HERBAL MENTAL HEALTH SUPPLEMENTS
SUBNICHES	BIOHACKS FOR PEOPLE WHO WANT SIX-PACK ABS INFORMATION PRODUCTS ON DEPRESSION IN TEENAGERS NOOTROPICS (BRAIN HEALTH SUPPLEMENTS) ORGANIC COLD REMEDIES FOR CHILDREN SCIENCE-BASED SUPPLEMENTS FOR SYMPTOMS OF MENOPAUSE TEA VARIETIES THAT LOWER BLOOD PRESSURE

Do you see how focused these subniches are? Many ecommerce businesses fail because they aren't specific enough. Get as detailed as possible when choosing your subniche.

SELECT YOUR SUB NICHE

- ORGANIC COLD REMEDIES
- TEA FOR BLOOD PRESSURE
- AROMATHERAPY FOR RELAXATION

SELECT YOUR PREFERRED MARKET

- HERBAL REMEDIES (NICHE)

HEALTH MARKET

Because I've mentored hundreds of people and talked to thousands of entrepreneurs, I'm positive that this is one of the most critical determinants of whether you're going to be successful in ecommerce. It's going to make the difference between you barely scraping by and being instantly profitable. It's the reason your prospects are going to choose YOU over the rest of your competition. This factor is why your business won't be a trend or a fad, but a legacy that's profitable far into the future.

And it's something that everyone in ecommerce seems to have missed.

But before you choose a final niche from that list, I have two critical questions to ask you.

Who do you want to solve problems for?

Consider exactly who you want to help. Will your ergonomic mouse for gamers work for people who have carpal tunnel? Will your potted plant business ship philodendrons and spider plants to first-time plant owners, or will you deliver rare orchids to collectors? Choosing the niche comes down to a single thing: thinking about your customers first. You will build long-term relationships with these folks.

Who do you want to build your business with?

How specifically are you going to help them? Ecommerce, and marketing in general, is the business of solving problems. And to build a business that lasts, your product must be the solution to a problem within your niche. Here is an example to show you how this works.

NICHE	PROBLEM	SOLUTION
GOLF CLUBS FOR KIDS	PARENTS DON'T BUY CLUBS FOR THEIR KIDS BECAUSE THEY ARE EXPENSIVE AND TOO LARGE. THE RESULT IS THE CHILD DOESN'T LEARN A PROPER SWING.	A LESS EXPENSIVE, CHILD-SIZED SET OF CLUBS FOR CHILDREN
BUSINESS PANTS FOR YOUNG FEMALE PROFESSIONALS	DRESS PANTS ARE UNCOMFORTABLE AND CAN BE UNFLATTERING BUT ARE NECESSARY FOR SOMEONE TO LOOK PROFESSIONAL.	A STRETCHY PANT WITH AN ELASTIC WAISTBAND THAT LOOKS LIKE DRESS PANTS BUT FEELS LIKE SWEATPANTS
BACKYARD BIRD WATCHING	FINCHES ARE SUSCEPTIBLE TO DISEASES FROM DIRTY FEEDERS.	AN INFORMATION PRODUCT AND CLEANING TOOL TO HELP CUSTOMERS PROPERLY CLEAN FEEDERS

As an Ecommerce Empire Builder, you are in the market of solving problems. And if you do that well, you'll get to the point where your customers will *need* to buy from you, because you're the only one who understands them and the only person who can solve their exact problem.

Before you choose, consider this bit of advice…

- You must stand by your niche 100%.
- If you feel wishy-washy about it, then it's not for you.
- If you think you'll grow bored of it in a year, you're in the wrong business.
- If you do not wake up excited to work on your business every day, you probably chose an unsuitable niche.

I believe in something called a **business-integrated lifestyle**. You shouldn't ever feel the need to run away from your business; you should actually enjoy what you do.

Now your niche doesn't have to be something you're an expert in…yet. Familiarity with your niche will absolutely help you, but it's more essential that it's something you truly care about. So many clients come to me for advice and immediately do $10K in sales their first month but then end up hating what they're selling.

If you choose something you feel passionate about, you will be much more willing to put in the time needed to become an expert.

When advising members of my Ecommerce Empire Builders course, I encourage them to first pick a niche based on intuition. So I'll ask you to do the same in this next exercise.

EMPIRE BUILDER EXERCISE

1. Revisit the list of 10 possible niches you wrote down earlier.
2. For each niche, list at least three subniches you are interested in pursuing. This will give you a total of 30 possibilities!

Niche	Subniche 1	Subniche 2	Subniche 3

3. Now go back and review each subniche again to see if it can be narrowed down further. Use the following criteria to adjust your choices so they are even more precise.
   - Age: What is the age group of your ideal customer?
   - Level of expertise: Will you serve beginners, intermediates, or experts?
   - Sex and/or gender: Is there a specific group you could solve problems for?
4. Now underline any subniches that will continue to inspire you five or even ten years from now. Which of these will have the kinds of customers you want to solve problems for?
5. Circle your overall favorite niche.

Now that you've chosen a market and found a niche you love, it's time to learn everything you possibly can so you can build your empire around it.

CHAPTER 3

UNCOVER YOUR NICHE

Research is a key component of your new business. Remember, an Empire Builder doesn't guess, incur unnecessary risk, or take chances. And the process of researching, or what I call **uncovering your niche**, will become the very foundation of your unbeatable offer. It's going to be the reason your customers come to YOU instead of your competition (like Amazon, Walmart, Etsy, and Shopify).

> The only way to compete with the giants in this industry is to solve problems for your customer better than anyone else.

To do that, you must get to know your customer. Now if you're already immersed in your niche because it's something that interests you, you are likely already a consumer in that space. For example, if your new ecommerce business is in the market of outdoor sports and the niche of paintballing, you probably already know what a butt pack is and what it means to "eat paint."

If you already read the content, buy the products, and follow the online forums, you are currently a consumer in your niche.

What you want is to become an *observer* in your niche. Pay close attention to what's going on. Think about the most recent product you bought in your niche.

- Why did you buy it?
- How was it marketed?
- Are there any ads for it on Google, Facebook, or YouTube?
- Why are you in a particular Facebook group or why have you subscribed to a certain YouTube channel?
- Are influencers already selling products in this niche? What do their ads look like?
- What attributes of the advertisements and content in this space do you like or dislike?

Take a birds-eye view of your niche to connect the dots and find out what's already working for your competition.

If you aren't already a consumer in your niche, why aren't you? This could be a sign that this isn't your ideal niche. If you aren't already excited in this space, go back to your list of 30 niches and choose something you already love.

Find problems in your niche.

You can find out exactly what problems you can solve for your niche through online research.

But first, you must know what to look for. One of the first things I did when I chose bass fishing as my niche was to really consider my customer base. I did that by answering a few simple questions to uncover their frustrations, fears, wants, and most importantly, their desires.

So what frustrates a bass fisher? When the fish aren't biting, of course. But also what are they afraid of? What keeps them up at night? What haunts and terrifies them?

You'll find that most people are afraid of failing. They are worried they won't catch that big fish and they'll lose credibility among their peers. Or they will take their kids on an expensive camping trip and everyone will be miserable.

So what do they want? They want to catch bigger bass, obviously. Or maybe a species they've never caught before. They want to know how to catch fish in any season and under a variety of conditions. They want to try out different types of flies.

But their desires? That goes deeper. It gets at the core of what everyone needs deep down. What does that angler want more than anything? Maybe it's to spend valuable time with their kids. Maybe it's to catch a bigger fish than their friend did. Perhaps they desperately long for a few quiet hours away from everything else that is going on in their life. Notice that a cool fishing lure isn't on their list of desires.

Now it's time for you to consider these questions in terms of your own niche.

EMPIRE BUILDER EXERCISE

Think about the people in your niche and answer the following questions.

My niche is:

- What are they frustrated by?

- What are they afraid of?

- What do they want?

- What do they desire?

Now that you have thought a bit about your ideal customer, it's time to do some research. So let's figure out where your people are hanging out online. Where do folks in your niche have real, authentic conversations with each other? Those honest discussions are a gold mine. You'll see their frustrations, fears, wants, and desires in every comment, post, and picture.

But that's not all you're going to find. You'll also notice new trends within the niche, which could help you anticipate a new, hot product before your competition does. In addition, you'll learn the lingo, which you're going to use when you create your funnel. So let's get you tuned in to your niche.

> **EMPIRE BUILDER EXERCISE**
>
> When I uncover a niche for a client or with a student, I have them create a folder on their computer or in a program like Dropbox or Google Drive so they can keep track of everything they learn.
>
> Create a folder called "Niche Research." In it, you'll record information in the following categories.
>
> - Influencers: Who is influential in your niche? These are the people who might help drive traffic to your funnel.
> - Competition: This is the group you'll learn from. They are going to teach you how to create advertisements and sell your product.
> - Indirect Competition: You could have a mutually beneficial relationship with these folks, as they sell products that are complementary to yours.
> - Trends: What are the latest trends in your niche? You will find out from these groups. Make sure to keep a list

handy, as you'll want to reference it when building out different offer types.

- Desires: What do your customers desire deep down? Maybe they want validation or a feeling of success. Maybe they want social affirmation through social media.
- Lingo: Vernacular in different niches is always changing. A new product or method will come around, and soon after, people will come up with new terms and phrases to talk about it. Make note of these, as you'll use them to build your funnel.
- Problems and Complaints: Here you can note people's frustrations, fears, wants, and desires that you find on these sites. You can even take screenshots of interesting conversations.

Add information to these folders as you continue to research your niche.

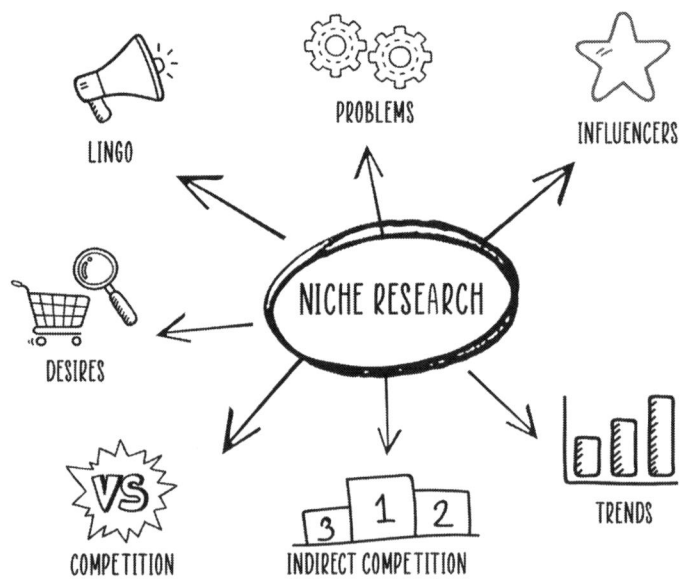

Now that you know what to look for, it's time to take a deep dive into your niche. There are nine steps to learning about your customer and your niche.

1. Familiarize yourself.
2. Find the influencers in your niche.
3. Identify direct and indirect competitors.
4. Pay attention to the trends.
5. Find out what they want.
6. Learn the lingo.
7. Find opportunity.
8. Note common problems and complaints.
9. Find out what they desire.

Step #1: Familiarize yourself.

Use the following platforms to familiarize yourself with your niche. Search within each site using your products' keywords.

Blogs

Check out some blogs in your niche. Simply type in one or two keywords for your niche + "blog." Just make sure to check the date of the most recent article, because many blogs out there haven't posted content in years.

Facebook Groups

There is a Facebook group for every niche, making this social media platform a great place to start. These groups are so popular that if your niche doesn't have one, you might have gotten *too* specific. Join a couple of groups to get a variety of perspectives, and look for ones with at least 5,000 members. A group with fewer members suggests there is not enough interest in this niche.

Instagram

Instagram is a great platform to pay attention to. While you won't find a ton of problems here, you will use it for other reasons. Instagram is where you can find key influencers and learn how to use beautiful imagery to showcase your products. Plus, it is an efficient way to see what sort of content your niche is currently consuming and a window into how others are already selling similar products.

Pinterest

Pinterest is another overlooked online community. Lots of ecommerce professionals see it as a space for women between the ages of 25 and 40 (and if that describes your customer, you absolutely *must* be on Pinterest). At its core, Pinterest is about providing content that solves problems, making it a particularly useful tool for you.

For example, when I type in "fly fishing," I find images illustrating how to tie different knots. See how that's a great solution to a problem? I bet you'll be surprised by all the useful content.

Reddit

Reddit groups are fantastic and totally underutilized. You can find the most authentic, honest conversations around your niche there. On this site, people share their excitement around a niche, talk trash about products, discuss the news, and share the items they like and use.

Threads in Reddit are called subreddits. You'll find your niche in one of these. Find a handful of subreddits in your niche and subscribe. I like to check in with my Reddit threads about twice a week.

YouTube

YouTube is a great place to understand how people are selling within your niche. How are people using helpful content (like how-to videos and tutorials) to sell similar products? How can you use video to sell your own products? Are there affiliate links or links to a funnel? Where does that link take you, and how can you use a similar strategy in your own funnel? Also, read some of the comments below the video. You can gain a lot of insight into what people want based on this feedback.

Other Online Forums

Your niche probably has online forums that aren't on one of these major platforms. Look for sites where people are talking in your market. Similar to googling blogs, just type in a couple keywords for your niche + "forum." Fly fishing, for example, has the North American Fly Fishing Forum as well as regional and local groups.

Step #2: Find the influencers in your niche.

For every niche, there will be influencers in that space. Who is everyone listening to? Who are the experts in that area? They are probably creating social media posts and might also have a YouTube channel. They also will post regularly (likely daily) and have at least 10K followers. (Later, I'll teach you how to use influencers to drive traffic to your funnel. But for now, I just want you to locate these people.)

Subscribe to their YouTube channels, like their Facebook pages, and follow them on Instagram. Take note of who these people are, where they are hanging out, and how many followers and subscribers they have. Make sure to save this info in your Niche Research folder.

Step #3: Identify direct and indirect competitors.

A direct competitor is in your niche and sells the same product as you. For example, imagine you sell protein powder to bodybuilders. Your direct competition also sells protein powder to bodybuilders.

Indirect competition sells a product complementary to yours to the same niche. For example, you might sell weight-loss supplements and your indirect competition sells a workout program.

Most people in the ecommerce world have no clue who their direct and indirect competitors are. This puts them at a disadvantage because indirect competition consists of people you could potentially work with to cross-promote each other's products. And your direct competition is a gold mine of information. Anytime you want to research what kind of marketing strategies are working, what trends are out there, or even what text to use on your site, your direct competition can give you inspiration.

Right now, you may not know exactly what product you'll sell, but you're probably starting to form a few ideas. What products might be complementary? Who sells them? Once you choose a product, you can start adding competitor information as well. You'll use it for inspiration later when you create your advertisements.

Step #4: Pay attention to the trends.

There will always be new trends in your niche, and they are opportunities to discover new products. One of my most successful funnels was based on a new trend in fishing. For a while, frog fishing, or using frogs as bait for catching bass, became really popular. Fishermen (and women) can use frog-shaped lures that float on top of the water, shimmering and creating noise. This kind of disturbance aggravates the bass so they'll want to attack it.

Before this practice became popular, I noticed it on a feed I followed. So by the time people were ready to start buying the product, I was one of the first people selling it. I sold out in 12 hours and gained tens of thousands of customers. It was one of the best product jumps I ever had. And I would never have known about it if I hadn't been fully immersed in my niche.

Step #5: Find out what they want.

What does your niche want? For example, in fly fishing, my customers want to catch bigger fish or fish in different seasons. What are your customers trying to achieve? Save photos, posts, and comments that illustrate this concept. Reddit is a great place to "eavesdrop" on these conversations.

Also, head to Amazon and check out the five-star reviews. Here you'll gain insight into the features that people really like. (I'll cover this in more detail later.)

Step #6: Learn the lingo.

Have you ever listened to a couple of friends talk about their shared hobby? A mountain biker might mention their "fork bottoming out on that drop," a snowboarder might say their "board has too much camber for park," or a rock climber might complain about getting "sandbagged on a twelve." If you are unfamiliar with your friend's niche, you will have no idea what they are talking about. As I mentioned earlier, each one has its own unique vernacular.

While researching, take note of how people in that space talk to one another. Are there any words, acronyms, or phrases you don't understand? Take note of these, as you're going to use this language to write all of your copy, including product descriptions, funnel content, and email templates.

Step #7: Find opportunity.

Where in your niche do you see an opportunity? You may not be able to answer this question yet, and that's okay. But it's good to start considering what kinds of products are out there and whether any of them can be improved. Or perhaps the item itself is fine, but it needs to be sold with an information product to help customers use it.

Information products include e-books, worksheets, cheat sheets, video tutorials, instructions, reference guides, demos, and FAQ sheets.

Navigate back to Amazon and read those reviews. Is there anything you can improve? Take a screenshot of any reviews that are especially useful.

Step #8: Note common problems and complaints.

Now that you've checked out a few platforms, met your influencers, and looked at some Amazon reviews, you likely see recurring problems and complaints. In fly fishing, people are always complaining about tangled lines and lost flies. Take note of these problems, as you're going to use them to create an unbeatable offer.

Step #9: Find out what they desire.

Sometimes people in your niche will say exactly what they want. Is there something people wish they had that would help them get their desired result?

Remember, *desires* are different than *wants*. A fly fisher might want to catch more fish, but they might desire to beat their last record. A leatherworker might want to design a new type of shoulder strap, but they desire comments, likes, and shares when they post pictures of a new bag. A trail runner could want tips to enjoy running more, but what they desire is a fun, new family hobby.

Okay, so you've immersed yourself in your niche. You are hanging out in the right Facebook groups and forums. You are familiar with your future customers, and you've identified their frustrations, fears, wants, and desires. What's more, you've created your own treasure trove within your Niche Research folder, which you'll leverage to ensure that you solve problems in your niche better than anyone else.

Now it's finally time to choose your product.

CHAPTER 4

CHOOSE YOUR PRODUCT

This stage is perhaps the most critical step in building your Ecommerce Empire. I always say that those who succeed in selling online don't gamble. On the surface, this might appear to be true simply because consumers increasingly buy products on the internet over brick-and-mortar locations.

But how many pop-up retailers appear on your Facebook feed only to disappear the following month? With so many businesses totally missing the mark—I'm talking belly-up, just-lost-$20K-failed—it can absolutely feel like ecommerce success is akin to the likelihood of winning a slot machine pull.

Most ecommerce entrepreneurs *are* gambling. That's because they don't choose the right product. Often sellers will pick something based on a gut feeling or advice from someone else. Don't get me wrong, that's a great place to start. You selected a niche within your wheelhouse, so it makes sense to rely on intuition. But your instinct must be proven with data.

That's because you aren't a gambler with pockets full of cash to burn—you're a scientist conducting an experiment, remember?

I'm going to show you exactly how to reliably choose the right product. And frankly, my advice might surprise you.

I'm also going to tell you how to conduct the research needed to prove that gut feeling for free using tools already at your disposal, and even how to test it with as little financial risk as possible.

To start, you'll determine your initial product offer.

IDENTIFY YOUR INITIAL PRODUCT OFFER

Your initial product offer (IPO) is the physical or information product you'll sell. For now, think of your funnel as a series of offers you present, and your IPO is the item that people are buying. Whatever your market may be, your IPO must be desirable enough to draw in your audience.

While your IPO can be almost anything, it needs to adhere to the following rules:

- It must be in your niche.
- Buyers should need more than one.
- It must be proven.

And of course, there is one other factor that by this point shouldn't surprise you: you should choose a product that you'll enjoy selling. You see, we've had so many students hit it big with a viral product or a trend, make some money for a month or two, and then have sales completely drop off.

You are going to invest a lot of time and energy making your funnel, so it stands to reason that you don't want to choose a product that no one will want a month from now. And of course it's way more fun to build a business and solve problems for people with a product you would actually use yourself. With that in mind, let's dive into the other three requirements.

It must be in your niche.

By now I hope this point is obvious, but I can't understate the importance of sticking to your market! Do not try to sell a product you don't know or care about, even if it meets all the other criteria outlined in this chapter. For example, if your niche is fall flannel clothing for hikers, your IPO might be a flannel jacket. If your niche is in the information world, it might be an e-book or a course.

You are going to spend a huge amount of time learning about the product, conducting market research, and building a funnel. Do you really think you can sustainably put thousands of hours of work into a product that doesn't align with your niche?

Buyers should need more than one.

Consider products in your niche that are often bought repeatedly or in bulk. What will your customers consistently need more of?

We've had success with items like stickers, charcoal toothpaste, notebooks, fishing lures, supplements, arts and crafts supplies, kids' toys, and pet toys to name a few.

You might choose to sell flies over a fly rod because that one rod will be used for years, whereas the flies will inevitably end up snagged in a tree or in a fish's stomach. Buyers always need more flies.

Here are a few examples of specific niches and the types of products that have netted over $10,000 a month for my clients.

NICHE	IPO
BUSY PARENTS	PUZZLE FOR KIDS
CAMPING	CUSHION SEATS
CATS	CATNIP
ENTREPRENEURS	SUCCESS JOURNALS & FOCUS SUPPLEMENTS
FLY FISHING	FLIES
LARGE DOGS	STRONG CHEW TOYS
PAINTING	PAPER AND BRUSH SETS

It's okay to sell a product that isn't in recurring demand—it isn't a make-or-break situation. If you've already chosen an IPO and it doesn't meet this standard, that's fine…with a caveat—it still must be proven (which you'll learn how to do a couple pages from now).

Also, not everyone has a physical product to sell. Information products like e-books and courses are typically something people will only buy once. Though that doesn't mean they aren't profitable.

EMPIRE BUILDER EXERCISE

Make a list of (at least) 10 products in your niche that you might sell, especially those that consumers are likely to buy more than one of. Hold on to this list, as you'll reference it soon.

1.

2.

3.

4.

5.

6.

7.

8.

9.

10.

This brings us to the third requirement of an IPO.

It must be proven.

Proving a product is the process of researching similar items in your niche to see if they meet your criteria. One tool I use is so powerful it can tell you not only what product to sell but also who is most likely to buy it. It can even predict future trends. This resource can tell you exactly what consumers are looking for in a similar product. It's free and you can use it immediately.

I'm talking about Amazon.

If you know what to look for, you can learn just about anything and everything about a product that an expensive team of analysts could. And it only takes about 10 minutes. By using Amazon as a research tool, you can find out…

- Whether you chose a profitable product
- The types of products in your niche that are selling today
- The kinds of products in your niche that will likely sell tomorrow
- How to price your product
- What keywords to use to describe your product
- How to make your product better than the competition's
- Which product(s) to upsell to your customer

How To Prove Your Product For FREE On Amazon

To prove your product, start from Amazon and type in your niche's keywords. When I researched my supplement start-up, I simply typed in "supplements for focus."

Below is a list of some details you should look for. As you research more items, try inputting the data into a spreadsheet to compare.

- Product Type

    From your search results, what are the first items that pop up in your niche? What's selling and for how much? Are any of them something buyers will purchase on an ongoing basis? If so, they might make a good IPO.

    For my search of "focus supplements," I found lots of various supplements promising to boost cognitive ability. Any products that are consumed regularly or consistently broken or lost—like toys for kids or pets—might be profitable IPOs. Of course, something trendy can also work, like a clever camping chair that someone might want to buy in multiples to give away to friends and family.

    Take note of items labeled Amazon's Choice, which are featured and tend to be quite popular.

- Product Categories

    Now click on one item that interests you from the search results. At the top of the page above the product information, you'll notice a hierarchy of **product categories** from broad to more specific. What are the niche categories this product fits into?

    Fly-fishing items look something like this:

    > Sports & Outdoors > Sports & Fitness > Hunting & Fishing > Fishing > Lures, Baits, & Attractants > Flies > Wet Flies

Click on a few subcategories for 5 to 10 products within your market. This will give you insight into other products your customers are buying and maybe some new ideas.

- Price

  The **price** of each item is right at the top of the page in red. Noting how much items generally cost will help you set your own pricing and inform your profit margin later.

  Under "fly fishing," I found a range of prices for flies. The Best Sellers item sold for $30, which gives me a good indication of what I could theoretically charge for a similar product.

  Generally, I price products for what similar ones sell for on Amazon. However, it isn't enough to simply price match. Instead, you'll also add more value to your offers with high-perceived-value products.

- Frequently Bought Together

  Under the main product description you'll find the "**Frequently bought together**" section. Which products are usually purchased at the same time as your desired IPO? Any of these are an excellent starting point to brainstorm additional products you'll use to craft your unbeatable offer.

  The "Frequently bought together" listing for a dog harness niche might look something like this:

  Dog harness + leash + collar

  Consider whether any of these items might make great add-ons for your future funnel.

- Product Information: Customer Reviews

    Scroll down to the "Product information" section and check Customer Reviews to find the **overall star rating**. Do people like the product? A four- or five-star average is a positive sign. But even if a particular product has a lot of negative reviews, it doesn't necessarily mean you couldn't sell a similar item (as long as interest is high). Just make sure that whatever concerns people express about it are addressed or are a non-issue with your product.

    In this same spot, check out the **number of ratings** it has. If it scores high on the Best Sellers Rank, it likely has a lot of reviews. If the product only has a few reviews, it's a sign that it does not have market demand and likely isn't worth selling. Remember, there may be alternative listings with more reviews for the same product. To find out whether this is the case, simply search again.

- Best Sellers Rank

    Also in the "Product information" section, you'll find the **Best Sellers Rank**. Here you can see how popular a product is within various categories. As a general rule, if a product is ranked around 20,000, it transacts about 100 times a day. So what does that tell us? It means A) that people are buying the product, and B) there is traffic in that niche. This is an excellent sign. Go ahead and check out the ranking of similar products within your niche.

- Customer Reviews

    Scroll down the product page a bit more to find the actual **reviews** people have left about the product along with their star ratings (in the "Customer reviews" section). Sort to see the top reviews by choosing that option from the drop-down menu. This will provide the best and worst reviews that buyers found most helpful.

What specifically do people like about the product and what do they dislike? As you narrow down your list of potential IPOs, you'll want to dig a little deeper into user feedback. Buyer comments can help you design both your product and the user experience.

For example, if someone says they like the quality of the product but are annoyed at the long shipping time, you can intentionally maintain quality but find a product source that can ship more quickly.

- New Releases And Most Wished For

  Finally, click the Best Sellers tab at the top of the page and navigate to the New Releases and Most Wished For sections. Based on New Release items, you can gain a solid understanding of current trends that are transacting now. It's perfectly acceptable, even encouraged, to hop on any hot-selling item bandwagon.

  But I think that the Most Wished For category is even more illuminating. Here you can see products that people want but have not yet purchased.

  Think about that for a moment.

  There is a category on Amazon that will tell you the kinds of products that people will want to buy *in the future*. It's your own customized crystal ball, free of charge. If any of your potential IPOs appear in these lists, it's a good indication that there is a significant market for them.

EMPIRE BUILDER EXERCISE

Write down 20 different products in your niche that you think you could sell. In your EEB folder, create a spreadsheet called IPOs. From your Amazon research, record the following details:

- Product description
- Current price
- Related products (from "Frequently bought together" section)
- Overall star rating
- Number of reviews
- Best Sellers Rank
- Customer review info (such as features people like or dislike)
- General notes

Use product categories, New Releases, and Most Wished For info to get inspiration for additional IPOs.

Out of the 20 products, choose the one item that you are most excited to sell and highlight it.

Having a great product that you've proven will set you up for a successful business is great. But here's what is going to elevate you as an Ecommerce Empire Builder: you won't stop at choosing an IPO. In fact, that's only the first step of many to crafting an unbeatable offer.

Unbeatable offers generally include the main product as well as one or two additional "freebies" that are perceived as high-value to the customer but are low-cost to you.

Unbeatable offers include items such as these:

- Free low-cost bonus item with order
- Information products that help solve a problem
- Information that helps the buyer enhance their experience with your product
- Access to private Facebook Groups

You can generally think about sales angles as the positioning of your offer in the marketplace. Some of the most common options include…

- Free-Plus-Shipping
- Deep Discount
- Limited-Time Offer
- Percent To A Cause
- Testers Needed

Free-Plus-Shipping

In a free-plus-shipping offer, often abbreviated as F+S, the buyer pays only for shipping and receives the item at no additional cost. So how do you make a profit or at least break even?

Choose Your Product

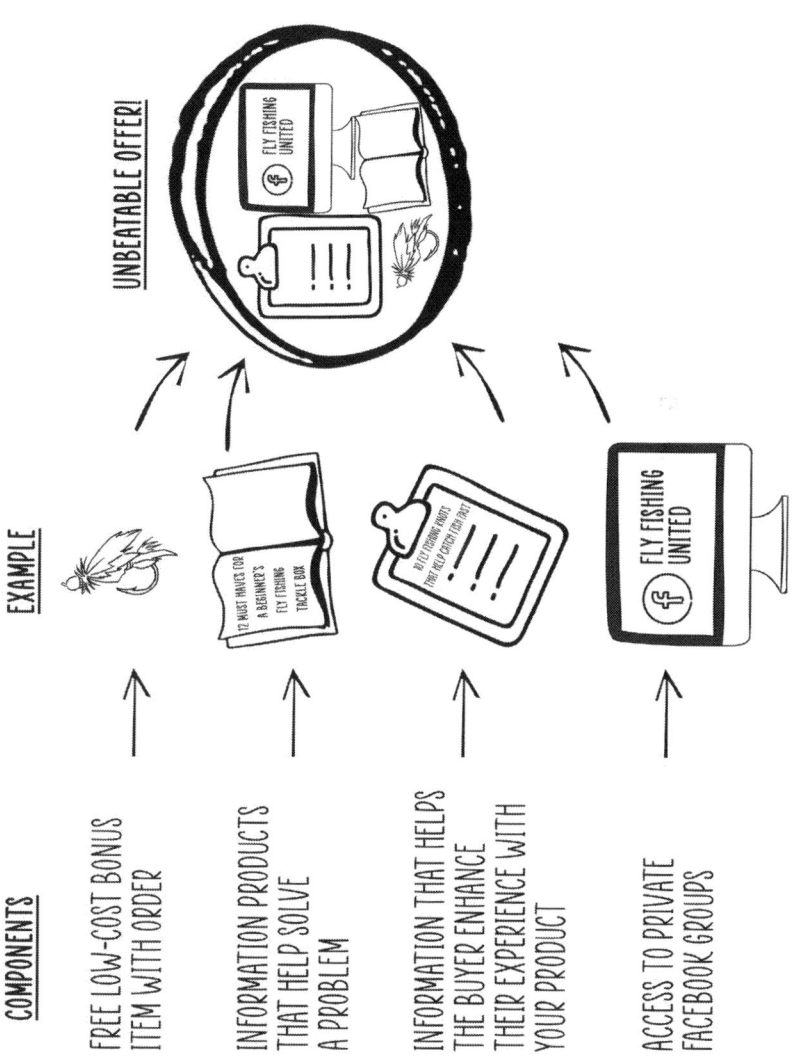

Because you'll purchase the item at a discount, you'll only pay a fraction of what someone else would. The amount you charge the customer should cover the cost of the item, the cost to ship, and if you choose your product source carefully, perhaps a small profit.

For example, in the niche of novelty coffee mugs, you might be able to purchase your mug for $2.99 and ship it for $3.99, or a total of $6.98. Your F+S offer could then sell the mug for $7.99, which is a reasonable cost to ship an item. And you would make $1.01 in profit.

That doesn't sound like much, but the goal of an F+S offer is not to make you instantly rich. Instead, it helps you use your IPO as bait to drive traffic to your funnel, where you then present additional products and offers to turn a more significant profit. In this system, the front-end product—the one that you're basically giving away—is called a loss leader.

Deep Discount

Another loss leader is a deep discount. Here instead of giving away the front-end product, you'll sell it at a premium. That is, you'll sell it for only slightly more than you paid for it. Alternatively, you could examine competitor prices and sell the product for less than anyone else in the market. Like with the free-plus-shipping model, you'll make most of your profit off additional products, subscriptions, or order bumps later in the funnel.

Often a deep discount is paired with an information product. For example, I could sell you fishing flies at cost, but include (for an additional fee) a fly-fishing guidebook. I could also include access to a private Facebook group or forum. Notice that these information products are low-cost to me, but have perceived high value to the customer.

Limited-Time Offer

Limited-time offers are created as a special package that will only be available for a specific period of time or until inventory runs out. They are a great way to test products and figure out whether they will sell, but they are also helpful to increase traffic for a short period of time. The power of this offer is in what is called scarcity, or the fear of missing out on getting the product.

If I were selling a limited-edition protein powder, I might say something like, "We have only seventy-two units of this limited-edition protein powder, and once it's gone, it might not come back again." Tempting, isn't it? If someone was already considering buying the product, this can often push them over the edge to a decision.

Percent To A Cause

Donating a percent of your earnings to a charity can help your customers overcome resistance to the sale. People feel good when they know their money is going to benefit others. Even better, you have the opportunity to help a charity you care about. It's really a win-win.

In my fishing business, we donated 10% of our proceeds to a program that helps special-needs children go fishing with their families by hosting events around the country. Our customers chose us over the competition in part because they wanted their money to do something meaningful.

This strategy can be especially effective if your offer isn't the cheapest on the market. For example, if I were selling a plush dog bed for 12% more than my competition, I might help my customers overcome opposition to that sale by donating 10% of the proceeds to the Humane Society. I would still earn a 2% higher price, the Humane Society would receive a 10% donation, and my customer would get a great product and the satisfaction of contributing to a cause we both care about.

Unfortunately, some people use this tactic to scam their customers by never actually making a contribution. This is not the kind of business owner you want to be. For one thing, if your customers ever learned you did this, your brand reputation would be ruined and you'd be out of business immediately. But most importantly, do you really want that kind of bad karma on your shoulders? Make sure you choose a charity that actually means something to you. And when you make that contribution, snap a photo of the check or the person you gave it to and post it on social media.

Testers Needed

This offer is similar to a free-plus-shipping system but with a twist. You'll break even on your front-end offer and profit off of upsells, subscriptions, or information products, but with the added benefit of receiving testimonials and feedback from your customers.

If I were testing out a new product for my DIY home renovation business, I might say something like, "New drill bits are in and we need product testers! If you agree to give us your feedback, we'll give you our new bits to try out. You just pay for shipping!"

This is an awesome way to pull customers into your world and expose them to your brand. You can ask them to submit written or video feedback along with photos of them using and enjoying the product.

Mix And Match

You can always combine these offers in different ways. For example, you might say…

> We just launched these five new flies, and we need people to battle test them!
>
> For a limited time only, we are giving away 200 sets to people willing to review these products.
>
> We'll send them to you for free. You just pay for shipping.
>
> But hurry—we're only offering them while supplies last!

So this offer combines Testers Needed with a Limited-Time Offer and Free + Shipping.

When you start building out your funnel, you'll see these types of offers interwoven into each page. We'll take a deeper dive into each one soon, but for now, just think about what kinds of offers might work best with your IPO.

EMPIRE BUILDER EXERCISE

1. What kind of offers and additional products might go well with your IPO? Jot down at least five ideas below.

    a.

    b.

    c.

    d.

    e.

    f.

2. What kind of unbeatable offers are already out there in your niche?

3. What kinds of products are your competitors bundling together?

4. Note the sequence of any ads that you would actually buy from.

5. Identify the elements of each ad that you find most compelling and add these to your EEB folder.

By now, you should have an IPO in mind. Make sure that this product is…

- Something you care about
- Within your niche
- An item that is bought repeatedly (or in multiples)
- Proven

If you haven't settled on an IPO yet, don't worry because in the next chapter you're going to learn how to source products. And as you'll soon see, some can be sourced more easily than others. Insight into where your product will come from may help you make the right choice.

CHAPTER 5

SOURCE YOUR PRODUCT

If you are completely new to ecommerce, it might surprise you to learn that you will not be creating this product yourself (unless it's an information product, like a book or a course). Instead, you'll work with a supplier that will source, store, and ship the product for you. For that reason, choosing a product and a supplier go hand-in-hand.

As you know, I got started in this business with Amazon's FBA. When I first heard about the program, I thought I had uncovered the secret to ecommerce success. Why? Because it is essentially a done-for-you program. All you have to do is source inexpensive inventory from a supplier, which you can find on websites like Alibaba.com. The product is then shipped to Amazon's warehouse, where they will store it for you (no inventory stashed in your garage!). Amazon will then list the product on their site, meaning you do not need to build a website or market your product. Then when someone buys the product, Amazon will ship it for you. They take a percent of the profit, and voilà—you're in the ecommerce biz. With this program, you don't have to do a thing. Sounds too good to be true, doesn't it?

As I told you, the business seemed like it could be profitable initially. I was on cloud nine...until I realized that my capital was *always* tied up in inventory. Building a business through Amazon is like playing in someone else's playground—you are essentially helping them build their empire instead of your own.

So when I began to rebuild, I knew I needed to have more control over my business. That's when I learned about something that changed my life: dropshipping.

Dropshipping essentially makes you the intermediary between the supplier and the customer. Your supplier handles fulfillment and shipping. All you have to do is market the product for them.

If you've never heard of dropshipping, just sit with that information for a moment, because it is truly revolutionary in the ecommerce world. The implications are tremendous.

You do not need to design or manufacture the product.

You do not need to store it.

You do not need to fulfill orders or drive to UPS several times a day.

You do not need to come up with a massive investment to begin.

Dropshipping is a low-risk and low-cost way to start an ecommerce business from scratch. It is the secret to my success and that of my students. It is a total game changer.

DROPSHIPPING BASICS

In the previous chapter, I gave you three rules to follow when choosing a product. But there is a fourth rule: the perfect product must be sourced through a supplier that will drop-ship the product for you. You don't want to invest a bunch of money on inventory. It's too risky. Especially if this is your first time creating an ecommerce business. Unless you are just dying to gamble between $10,000 and $20,000, in which case you might as well go to a casino.

You see, you might try out 10 different IPOs and mix and match them with 30-some upsells before you find a winner. The odds are stacked against you that you'll hit the jackpot on your first try.

Instead, I'm going to show you how to keep your initial costs as low and risk-free as possible. You won't have to buy a ton of product. You're not going to ship it. And you won't be diving into the market without a test drive.

Dropshipping works like this:

1. A customer goes to your funnel.
2. They make a purchase.
3. You collect payment and shipping details from the customer.
4. You contact your supplier.
5. The supplier ships the product to your customer.
6. You take a cut of the profit.

    Bonus: Steps 4 and 5 can be automated!

Let's say you charge a customer $20 for your kit. You take that money, go to the supplier, the supplier charges you $10, and you make $10.

As you become more sophisticated and scale your business, you can start tweaking and branding your own products. But for now, this method is going to be the easiest to get started.

Suppliers

So what makes a good supplier? Any business that will store and ship your product. You could easily use products from Amazon, Walmart, or Etsy, put them into a great funnel, and BOOM—you've just created a drop-shipping ecommerce biz.

For example, I could sell fishing flies from Amazon, pair each one with a guide book, and offer a subscription. Remember, you're just marketing the products. However, to be profitable, you likely want to work with a supplier or manufacturer so you can get the best price.

Most ecommerce drop-shipping businesses start with the biggest company you've never heard of: Alibaba. Alibaba is basically the Amazon of the world. The Alibaba Group is China's largest online commerce company. Its sites have hundreds of millions of users and host millions of merchants and businesses. During the time we wrote and published this book, Alibaba was handling more business than any other ecommerce company. Their website helps to connect exporters in China (and other countries) with companies in over 190 countries around the world.

Both Alibaba and AliExpress allow anyone from anywhere to source products from China (and a few other countries) and arrange to have those products drop-shipped to their customers. Alibaba offers products direct from suppliers, while AliExpress is more like a directory of suppliers that offer dropshipping.

Prices on these sites are often dramatically lower than what you'd find on Amazon or Walmart because the products are direct (or very close to direct) from the manufacturer. And the price continues to drop based on the number of units purchased. The best part is that with dropshipping, you don't have to buy product in bulk. In fact, most will let you purchase one item at a time as customers order them.

> **EMPIRE BUILDER EXERCISE**
>
> 1. Head to AliExpress.com or Alibaba.com.
> 2. Type in a product you'd like to sell. If you don't already have an IPO in mind, just type in any product.
> 3. Compare the price of that product to what it sells for on Amazon.

At the time I was writing this book, a set of 40 flies in a case was selling for $40 on Amazon, while the same exact product was available on Alibaba for between $2.20 and $3.40 a case, depending on how many units you purchased. From both of these sites, you can also see items that are often bought together, which you can use to create upsells in your funnel.

VET YOUR SUPPLIERS

Now that you've identified a product you might want to sell from Alibaba or another supplier, it's time to vet that supplier and product. Generally, I'll look at a few key indicators on sites like Alibaba, and if I'm interested in doing business with that company, I'll contact them directly. Below are a few metrics I suggest you check

Read the reviews.

Check out the product reviews. Do customers have any serious complaints about product quality? Keep in mind that there will be at least a few fulfillment-based complaints for all products, specifically around slow shipping times or broken items. If someone purchases 10,000 units, a handful are bound to be broken or arrive late. However, if customers routinely find product defects or have concerns around quality, that should be a red flag.

Check the supplier's ranking.

Sites like Alibaba rank suppliers based on customer ratings. Generally, you'll look for a supplier with a high ranking across categories such as shipping, communication, and product quality. Also check for any sort of trust badges that have been awarded.

Note experience.

Look for metrics that indicate the supplier's level of experience. For example, on Alibaba, I look at the dollar amount of transactions over a period of time. If a supplier has only been around for about a year or if they've only done a couple hundred bucks in transactions, that's a strong indicator that they aren't very experienced. Look for a supplier that has been working in the space for at least three to four years.

Look at the response rate.

A high response rate is indicative of a professional. You will want to talk directly with your supplier at some point, for example if something is wrong with the product or you want to negotiate terms. So it's good to know that you can expect a timely response.

Determine whether they are a manufacturer or trading company.

A trading company is essentially a go-between for you and the supplier. Ideally, you'll work with a manufacturer directly. Remember, you want to keep your costs as low as possible, which means working directly with the source. That way, you'll likely get the best price, with the added bonus of being able to speak directly to the company you source products from.

However, I encourage you not to order off the site where you found the supplier. Instead, do a little digging and contact the supplier yourself. If you do, you can negotiate a way better deal. And you'll have the added advantage of working directly with the supplier. This is a critical relationship to build because you might want to make changes to the product once your funnel becomes profitable.

Remember, this initial product offering is just your starting point. Once you've transacted $10K for three consecutive months, you're going to brand the product. And to do that, you'll need to build a relationship with that supplier.

But I'm getting ahead of myself. First, let's look closer at those suppliers.

> **EMPIRE BUILDER EXERCISE**
>
> To vet a potential supplier, look for a link to their website, a phone number, or an email address. Contact at least three suppliers you would consider working with. I recommend sending them a picture of what you'd like to sell (you can just use the same photo they used for the product listing) and ask for a quote on 500, 1,500, and 2,000 units.
>
> When they message you back, you'll see how dramatically the price varies between low and high volume. The higher the volume, the better your margins. Be sure to request a catalogue of all their products. There you might find a product you like better, or a few items that would work as upsells.

LIMITATIONS OF ALIBABA AND ALIEXPRESS

If you drop-ship with Alibaba, you will have to deal with long shipping times. And your customers won't always be happy about it. But there are two things you can do to help things go a little more smoothly.

- **Overcommunicate to your customer during this time.** Some of them will want a refund, and it's no big deal. Others will just want to know what is going on. Make sure you are in communication with them throughout this process.
- **Get something in their hands immediately.** You can ease a lot of stress around slow shipping times by sending them something while they're waiting for the main product. This might be a digital product they can start using right away, like an e-book, a cheat sheet, or a video course. For example, if I were selling cookware, I might email them a

recipe e-book. That way, they can learn about it ahead of time and immediately start using their purchase once they receive it.

UNDERSTANDING PRICE

Now that you've contacted a few suppliers, let's compare those quotes. To do so, you'll have to consider the product cost and the cost of shipping.

For example, one set of fishing flies on AliExpress breaks down like this.

QUANTITY	PRODUCT COST	SHIPPING	YOUR TOTAL COST
X1	$9.06	$2.63	$11.69
X2	$18.12	$2.63	$20.75
X4	$36.24	$2.63	$38.87
X6	$54.36	$2.63	$56.99
X8	$72.48	$2.63	$75.11

Now you want your customers to buy multiple units, and I'll show you why in the following chart. To incentivize them to do this, the cost per unit will go down for each one they order. Why would you do that? The more product your customer buys, the more your margins increase. You're going to pass that deal on to your customers and get more profit as well.

You can play around with different multipliers to change the percentage that the customer saves by buying in bulk. You'll also notice that the shipping rate stays the same per unit.

Here's how I like to price my front-end offer.

Total Cost x Profit Multiplier = Customer Total

QUANTITY	COST + SHIPPING	PROFIT MULTIPLIER	SALE PRICE
1	$11.69	3	$35.07
2	$20.75	2.5	$51.88
4	$38.87	2.1	$81.63
6	$56.99	1.8	$102.58
8	$75.11	1.5	$112.67

See how much more value the customer gets as they purchase more units? You want to incentivize them to buy multiple units, so it's vital to give them a better and better deal. Here's where the magic comes in: you're also getting a better deal!

Let's subtract our cost + shipping from the sale price.

QUANTITY	COST + SHIPPING	PROFIT MULTIPLIER	SALE PRICE	PROFIT
X1	$11.69	3	$35.07	$23.38
X2	$20.75	2.5	$51.88	$31.13
X4	$38.87	2.1	$81.63	$42.76
X6	$56.99	1.8	$102.58	$45.76
X8	$75.11	1.5	$112.67	$37.56

Your customers are getting a great deal and you are making as much money as you can. It's truly a win-win.

EMPIRE BUILDER EXERCISE

Depending on your product, you'll likely find many different suppliers selling essentially the same thing.

1. Compare similar products from different suppliers. Which one gives you the best deal?
2. Go ahead and play with your profit multipliers too.
3. To get an idea of what your initial sale price should be, check out what similar items are selling for on Amazon.

CHAPTER 6

DESIGN YOUR SALES FUNNEL

When I started to rebuild my business, I knew I needed a platform different from Amazon's FBA. I was aware of various kinds of online storefronts like WooCommerce and Shopify, so I decided to start drop-shipping on one of them. Through Facebook ads and social media influencer shoutouts, I finally had customers. I was making sales. Actually, I was making about $20,000 a month.

Time to celebrate, eh?

Not quite.

I was actually *losing* three cents on every transaction. What was I doing wrong? I knew that other people were finding success with ecommerce, so why was I in the red? I had a great product in a niche I cared about. I had control over my business and had found a great supplier who could drop-ship for me. So what was the problem?

Ever since college, I had been in business mastermind groups. I just love investing in myself. So even though I didn't have much money at the time, I was in an entrepreneurial mastermind, which was basically a group for sellers on Amazon. During one weekly meetup, the host of the mastermind mentioned a newly-launched sales-funnel software.

I wondered, *Where has this been all my life?!*

It was like learning the dark arts of internet marketing. Instead of my customer being bombarded with a bunch of different products and offers, and me competing with those offers, I had complete control over what they saw at every step of the process.

From the moment they landed in my funnel to the thank-you page and the follow-up emails, sales funnels allowed me to be in complete control of my product sales process. And that's when my business went from losing money with each transaction to earning me between $5,000 and $10,000 a month in net profit.

Aliakbar Gulshan was one of the first mentees inside my Empire Builder course. He hit our 10K club, which happens when you earn $10K in sales each month, within his *first month*. Now he's in my most elite group—my Inner Circle program—made up of entrepreneurs growing to reach the seven-figure mark quickly. In 2019, Ali helped me launch Untapped Focus, the first all-natural performance enhancer designed specifically for entrepreneurs.

Before we met, Ali had had a devastating ecommerce experience as well, but it was through Shopify. Unlike me in my first venture, Ali already knew about dropshipping. However, Shopify was the only platform he knew how to do it on. He allocated about $200 of an initial investment for each product to pay for product testing, buy ads, and set up stores. He tried dozens of products. And every single time, he lost more and more money.

But he told himself the method was right; he was just choosing the wrong product. (This is why we prove our niche!) So he watched more tutorials and bought a few more Shopify apps to help him monitor his business.

One day, he had a pop-up from an app that managed his bills notifying him that he was in the red. You see, Ali had been on a free trial of Shopify and it had come to an end. But he was steadfast in his resolve, convincing himself that he could make the money back.

Ali is a marketing genius. So despite having a small budget, he was able to drive people to his site using influencer traffic. He watched Google Analytics like a hawk, closely monitoring how many people were navigating to his site. They were coming in, so he figured the money would too.

But when prospects started buying, he still couldn't cover the cost of marketing and overhead.

> Ali will tell you, and I agree with him, that Shopify and FBA and Etsy and all these other platforms have a place in the ecommerce ecosystem. They can be valuable, nearly passive revenue streams. But he'll also tell you that they aren't the right solution for somebody just getting started. And even for an experienced ecommerce business owner, they are only one piece of the revenue stream.

In the red, losing 10 cents on every dollar, Ali was desperate.

His Shopify account was free, but he had to buy so many Shopify apps to run the business that he was spending about $300 a month just to use the platform.

That's when Ali stumbled onto one of my YouTube case studies. (If you want to check it out, head over to EcommerceEmpireBuilders.com/Kickstart to get the case study.) In this video, I launched a funnel for a product I was unfamiliar with and made $700 in the first day.

Soon after, Ali started using sales funnels. But he left his Shopify account up, wanting to have a fallback in case this new method didn't work for him. He built a funnel that looked like an online storefront, but streamlined it and took away unnecessary distractions.

Meanwhile he was still sending traffic to his Shopify store. It was converting at only about 1%, and even worse, wasn't even breaking even.

But his funnel? It started converting at a whopping 15%! And that's just for his IPO. Ali didn't even know about all the other secrets I'm about to show you, like upsells and continuity.

What Ali realized was that he had a great product and he was selling in the right niche. The problem wasn't his customers or his product, it was the platform. He also realized (and if you're using Shopify or Amazon right now, this will definitely speak to you) it wasn't that he couldn't make enough sales. He had been agonizing over how to get more people to buy. The real problem was that he was being gouged on every single sale.

HOW TO CHOOSE A PLATFORM

If you use Shopify, you might be saying, "Pete, I can have funnels in Shopify!" Technically you're correct. But it's expensive, at $50 a month plus a 3% transaction fee. If that's what you want to do, that's completely fine. It truly doesn't matter what platform you use, as long as it works for you. Here's what you should look for in a funnel platform.

- **Fewer options (less competition)**

    Let's say you're in the surfing niche and you sell board shorts. If you were to place your IPO on a Shopify store, you would be competing with hundreds of other board shorts. Do you really want to contend with all those other dropshippers and manufacturers?

    When you create a funnel, your prospect only sees one item, and it's yours. So your customer won't have to wade through a ton of other products, and they won't be distracted by a bunch of buttons.

- **Reasonable price**

    A sales funnel platform won't take a percent of every transaction. Instead, they opt for a flat-rate model in which you make a monthly payment. Within that fee, they usually include a funnel template, basic email marketing, and payment integration. Other platforms like Shopify offer a lower monthly fee (to entice new users) but quickly eat into profits by taking a significant percent of sales.

- **Resistance-free sales**

    One of my first jobs was selling televisions at Circuit City. Folks would come in looking for a TV, but they'd leave with an upgraded model, universal remote, Blu-ray player (this was the 2000s, after all), and a warranty, and they'd have it all shipped to their home.

    But all they wanted originally was a flat-screen. So what happened?

    Nothing nefarious, to be sure. On the contrary, they went to a store looking for a specific product, and then a skilled salesperson showed them how and why these complementary products would benefit them.

But without that face-to-face interaction, how do you create that kind of experience online?

The answer is *not* through Amazon or Shopify. For one thing, with those platforms, any additional items are added *before* people check out. That means they can see the cart total increasing again and again, and then BOOM—you've lost your prospect.

Why don't shoppers just avoid salespeople? Well for one, it's much ruder to walk (or run) away from an actual person than an online cart. And two, it's because they aren't constantly reminding you of how much more each item will cost. Imagine if a salesperson did some quick math to give you an updated price every time you added an upgrade. They wouldn't make much on commission!

A funnel, on the other hand, processes the payment for the initial IPO and then, with one click, automatically charges the card for any additional purchases, creating an experience much closer to face-to-face sales than to typical online transactions.

- **Multi-product funnels**

The last major advantage to using funnels instead of more traditional online storefronts is the profitability of multi-product sales. For example, usually online businesses just sell a single product, one at a time. The result is an average cart value that is likely…well, average. This one is so powerful, it deserves its own section.

MULTI-PRODUCT FUNNELS

Let's imagine you sell an item for $3.97 plus shipping and you sell 500 of them in a month. The majority of your buyers will typically buy just that one item. To figure out your gross profit, you just multiply $3.97 by 500 orders to get $1,985. Not so profitable, eh? In that scenario, you'd be lucky to break even once you factor in the cost of marketing, product cost, and other expenses.

But what happens if you sell more than one product?

Now what if you were able to show your customer that the more they buy, the better the deal? That's a multi-product funnel, and it can dramatically increase your revenue. Check out what happens if the majority of those customers buy four units instead of just one.

AVERAGE CART VALUES
MULTI-PRODUCT

ITEM
- 1X BUZZIN' FROG
- 2X BUZZIN' FROG (DIFFERENT PATTERNS)

MOST POPULAR!
- 4X BUZZIN' FROGS (DIFFERENT PATTERNS)

- 6X BUZZIN' FROGS (DIFFERENT PATTERNS)
- 8X BUZZIN' FROGS (DIFFERENT PATTERNS)

500 ORDERS
11% - 55 ORDERS - $218.35
24% - 120 ORDERS - $956.40
38% - 190 ORDERS - $2,844.30
21% - 105 ORDERS - $2,306.85
6% - 30 ORDERS - $899.10

TOTAL: $7,225 / 500 = $14.45

When you sell multiple units, your revenue increases, even though your traffic stays the same. Notice that only 11% of customers opted for a single unit. But 24% bought two, 38% bought four, 21% bought six, and 6% bought eight units. Suddenly, your average monthly gross profit jumps to $7,225 with an average cart value of $14.45 per transaction. That's nearly 4X the lame single-item purchase profits!

Let me just pause here to remind you that this a real-world example. And our clients get these same results, so you can too!

The profitability of multi-product funnels is particularly underscored when you consider the cost to acquire each of those customers. Remember, traffic to your funnel won't be free. Whether you pay Facebook, Google, or an influencer to get potential customers in, there will be a cost.

Based on my experience and that of my students and clients, it costs around $5 for someone to take a free-plus-shipping offer.

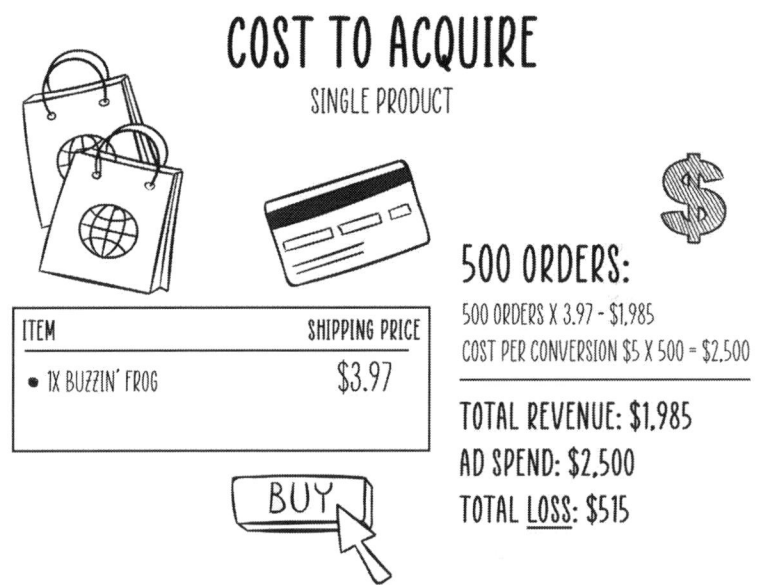

When you multiply the cost per conversion of $5 times 500 customers, you spend $2,500 to get those buyers into the funnel. And when you subtract your cost per conversion from your revenue, you come up with a LOSS of $515.

So many clients come to me because they are losing money with every sale. Or worse, some think they are making money because they can see the revenue, but they neglect to consider the cost of each sale.

Let's take a closer look at the multi-product option.

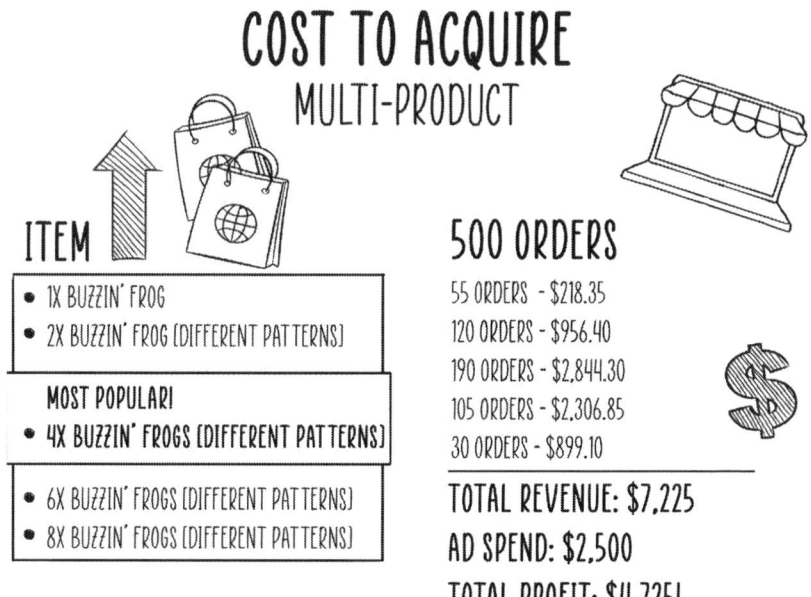

COST TO ACQUIRE
MULTI-PRODUCT

ITEM
- 1X BUZZIN' FROG
- 2X BUZZIN' FROG (DIFFERENT PATTERNS)

MOST POPULAR!
- 4X BUZZIN' FROGS (DIFFERENT PATTERNS)

- 6X BUZZIN' FROGS (DIFFERENT PATTERNS)
- 8X BUZZIN' FROGS (DIFFERENT PATTERNS)

500 ORDERS
55 ORDERS - $218.35
120 ORDERS - $956.40
190 ORDERS - $2,844.30
105 ORDERS - $2,306.85
30 ORDERS - $899.10

TOTAL REVENUE: $7,225
AD SPEND: $2,500
TOTAL PROFIT: $4,725!

Your cost per conversion stays the same at $5, so the total ad spend to get those customers will remain $2,500. If you subtract the ad spend from the total revenue of $7,125, you have a total profit of $4,725. To turn this offer into a profitable one, all you had to do was offer bulk orders. That's a pretty simple change to make, considering it increased profit by 817%!

FUNNEL FUNDAMENTALS

Learning how funnels operate will open your eyes to the possibilities of making tremendous amounts of money in the ecommerce space. A sales funnel is a guided step-by-step process you take your customer through. It has the benefit of making your business the most revenue while also giving your customer the best possible experience.

Your customer is moved through a funnel, a sequence of offers that are tailored to present solutions to their problems through your products. You understand your customer so well that you know exactly what kind of offer will help them, therefore you can also suggest additional related products that will improve their experience.

Meanwhile, you are going to make the most money possible because you won't use a platform that takes a significant share of the transaction, and because you are creating an unbeatable offer.

If you've already started an ecommerce biz on Shopify, Amazon, WooCommerce, or a similar platform, you'll have to go through a mindset shift to get on board with funnels. Unlike a traditional online storefront, you aren't just going to reveal a single offer and be done with the transaction. (Or as I always like to say, just because you think you're done selling doesn't mean your customer is done buying).

For example, when a customer comes into my fishing funnel, they rarely purchase a single set of flies and then leave. Why is that? Partly because of the power of multi-product offers, and also because of a series of additional offers that I know would likely benefit them.

A funnel has a few basic components, which include...

- Opt-in/sales page
- Order plus quantity breaks and order bumps
- Multiple upsells
- Thank-you page

This is not an exhaustive list—funnels can be much more complicated. But these are the most critical pages for an ecommerce sales funnel.

Each of these pages is carefully designed with a specific purpose, with the end goal of growing your business assets, current sales, and future sales. On many platforms, these pages will be built for you—you just have to provide the sales copy and images.

Your funnel might not look exactly like this one, but this is the structure I've found to be the most effective after years of testing.

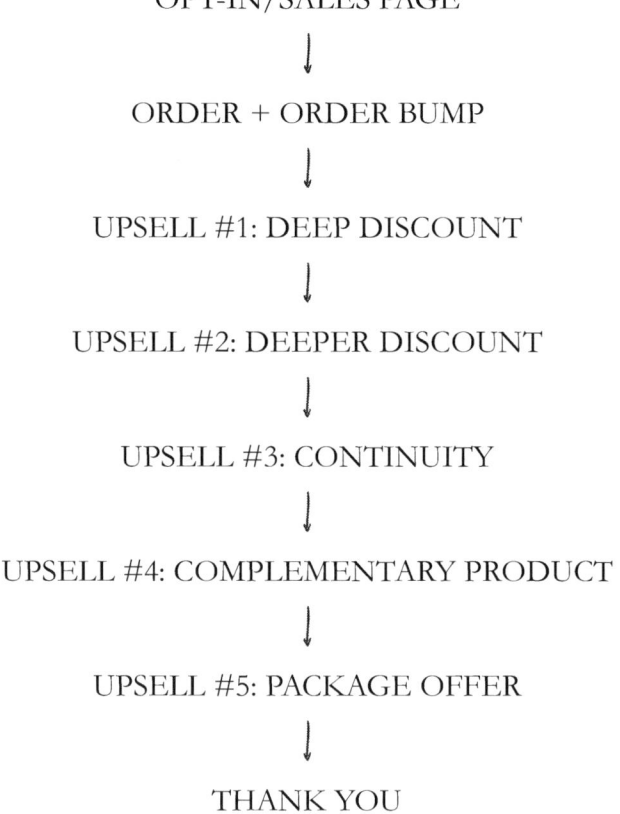

Here's a general overview of how all the pieces work together.

Opt-in/Sales Page

The opt-in is the first step of the funnel. For the viewer to pass through to the order, they first need to opt in by providing their email address. This is critical because the most profit is gained on the back end, after the initial product offer. Their email address is key to repeat business. Once they input it, they are sent to the order page.

Order Page + Order Bump

On the order page, your customer will input their billing and shipping information and select the number of units they'd like to purchase. Then the magic happens.

An order bump is essentially when a prospect pre-purchases an inexpensive additional item. This sounds confusing, but it's actually very simple. When you're checking out at the grocery store, see a pack of gum at the register, and toss it into the cart, that's an order bump. It's a quick, inexpensive item that a customer can easily toss in the cart without much thought or hesitancy.

For example, a $1 tin of mints is an excellent order bump because the low cost creates little resistance to the sale, whereas a $50 pair of sunglasses likely wouldn't be an easy choice. In the ecommerce world, order bumps include items like limited-edition versions of the product, expedited shipping, and e-books.

> **Note: An order bump is technically a type of upsell. The distinguishing characteristic is the point in the funnel at which each takes place. An order bump always happens *before* the payment info is captured. You can think of an order bump as a pre-purchased upsell. In contrast, your upsell pages always appear *after* the first purchase is made.**

Upsells

Most of your funnel will consist of various types of upsells, which could be any of these:

- A small, inexpensive item
- The same item they just bought but at a better price
- Complementary products
- Information products
- A package deal
- A subscription
- A service

You can have as many upsells as you wish, although I have found the perfect number that works best for my funnels. (Don't worry—I promise to share that with you later!) Regardless of the number of upsells you integrate into your funnel, each one should be accessible by a single click and not take them back to their cart.

Why? Because you want to make it easy for the customer to move through your funnel, and also because if they see their total cost dramatically increasing as they purchase more items, they might leave altogether.

Funnels don't use cart pages like traditional stores do. Cart pages tend to result in a lot of buyer's remorse, and this is one of the main reasons that storefronts have such small conversion rates as compared to funnels.

Here are a few different types of upsells.

- **Deep Discount:** This is an offer to buy the same product but at a better price. Who wouldn't want more of what they just bought for less money?
- **Continuity:** At least one of your upsells should include continuity, meaning that the buyer purchases some kind of subscription where they'll be billed monthly for the service. To see the types of products and features typically used for subscriptions and determine how this type of program might fit with your particular business, check out MySubscriptionAddiction.com.
- **Complementary Items:** Remember the additional items you researched that were on the Most Wished For and Best Sellers pages on Amazon? These will make great upsells for additional products that can be used with your IPO. (The Frequently bought together section is a great place to find complementary items too.)

Thank-You Page

After the upsell series, you might think this is the end of making money in your funnel. But no—this final page is actually going to include another offer.

As you can see, your funnel will be relatively simple, with about eight different pages, all designed to create a streamlined buying experience for your customer. You'll mix and match different types of upsells with your sales page, order page, and thank-you page to create a truly unbeatable offer.

Here's an example of a fishing funnel.

OPT-IN

Here we collect the customer's email address so we can follow up with offers and marketing content later.

ORDER + ORDER BUMP

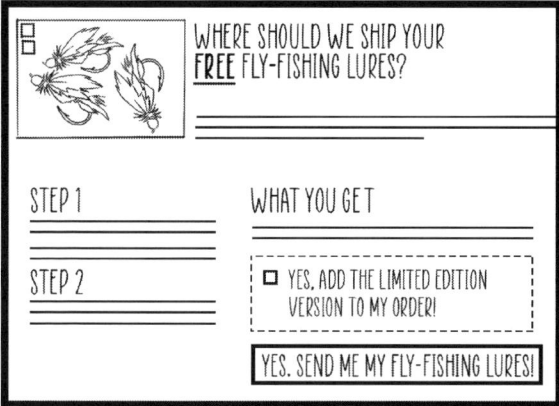

On our order page, we display the IPO (a box of flies) and the price of a single unit plus multiple units (quantity price breaks). You'll also notice on this page that the customer can see our order bump, incentivizing them to purchase a small case for their flies.

↓

UPSELL #1: DEEP DISCOUNT

For upsell number one, we offer a deep discount of four more boxes of flies at 20% off the initial IPO price.

↓

UPSELL #2: DEEPER DISCOUNT

For our second offer, we'll do an even deeper discount than the first upsell. Now they have the opportunity to purchase two more additional units at 30% off the price listed on the order form here.

UPSELL #3: CONTINUITY

The continuity upsell is a chance to join our Fly Fishing United club, where they can pay monthly for a subscription that delivers fly-fishing equipment to their door every month. (And we get to bill them $29.97 each of those months!)

UPSELL #4: COMPLEMENTARY PRODUCTS

Here we offer a complementary product of a fishing net. Remember, your customer doesn't just need your IPO, they want everything they'll need to achieve their desired result. And I know that if my customers are going to reliably reel in fish, they'll need a net to get the fish out of the water.

UPSELL #5: PACKAGE OFFER

Next, I have a package offer of a multi-tool set so my customers can make simple fixes to their equipment while outdoors. Again, if I stopped selling at flies, my customers wouldn't have every tool they need to achieve their end result. That's why I'm continuing to offer them products that will help them be successful.

THANK-YOU PAGE

Here, we confirm the customer's order, delivery and info bonuses, and link them to any other offers we might have.

Again, you can mix and match and add or subtract upsells to create an offer that makes sense. For example, a dog-training business with an IPO of a specially designed harness might look something like this.

OPT-IN

ORDER + ORDER BUMP

↓

UPSELL #1: DEEP DISCOUNT

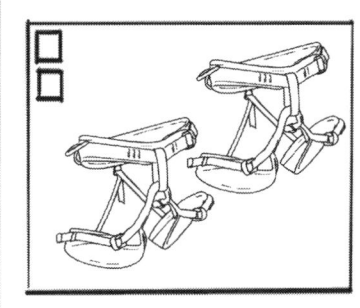

SECOND HARNESS AT 20% OFF!

YES! UPGRADE MY ORDER NOW
JUST $9.97 (REGULAR PRICE $34.99)

↓

UPSELL #2: PACKAGE OFFER

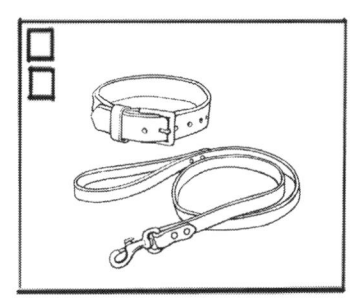

ADD TWO DOGGIE SEATBEALTS AND TWO LEASHES!

YES! UPGRADE MY ORDER NOW
JUST $4.97 (REGULAR PRICE $24.99)

UPSELL #3: CONTINUITY

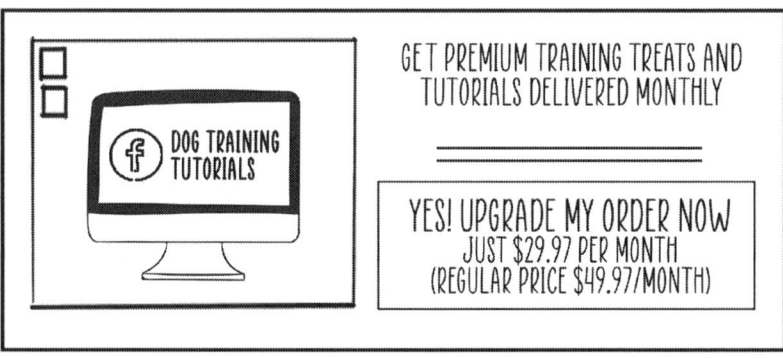

UPSELL #4: COMPLEMENTARY PRODUCTS

↓

UPSELL #5: PACKAGE OFFER

ADD A PREMIUM BOOK ON
HOW TO SAFELY INTRODUCE DOGS TO CATS

YES! UPGRADE MY ORDER NOW
JUST $29.97 (REGULAR PRICE $49.99)

↓

THANK-YOU PAGE

See how you can mix and match upsells in your funnel to create an offer tailored to your niche? This eight-page format has been the most successful for me and my students. However, you should try out different funnel structures to figure out which one works best for your business and products.

Also, be careful not to choose too many different products. The fewer you offer, the fewer customer support emails, product costs, and headaches you'll have to deal with. Besides, if you offer 10 or 20 different products, you'll have a harder time figuring out which one is moving the needle for your business.

Remember, you're a scientist conducting an experiment; therefore, you need to limit your variables. When you're ready to grow, instead of adding more products to your existing funnel, you'll build a new funnel with new IPOs and upsells.

Another advantage to funnels is that the basic structure will stay the same as you test out different products. Your IPO might change; therefore, your order bump and deep discount upsells may change as well, but unless you change your niche, the continuity piece as well as any complementary products and your thank-you page will stay the same.

This way, once you have your first funnel built out, you can easily swap out various pieces of the puzzle without doing any major structural change to your business.

FUNNEL ECOSYSTEM & BUSINESS FUNDAMENTALS

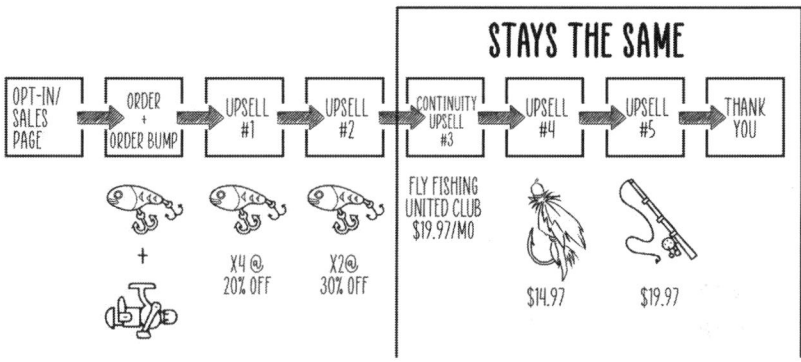

INTEGRATING AN UNBEATABLE OFFER INTO A WINNING FUNNEL

Now that you understand how a funnel works and have chosen an IPO and identified potential upsells, let's take a closer look at how to combine all these factors into an unbeatable offer.

If you're building out a funnel for the first time, I recommend integrating two sales angles into your offer: free-plus-shipping and deep discounts.

With a free-plus-shipping offer, the great deal you offer on your IPO will pull prospects into your funnel. Then you'll make most of your profit through upsells later in the funnel. Earlier, I mentioned that this strategy is called a loss leader, which suggests that you'll lose money on the IPO.

But in reality, you'll break even (or possibly make a little profit), even if the customer declines any upsells.

The main reason I like this strategy is that it's so easy to start making sales with this model. As you gain more loyal customers, you may want to start playing around with IPO offer strategies. But right now, one of the easiest ways to entice someone to give up their contact information and become familiar with you and your business is to craft an offer they simply can't refuse.

Sometimes the cost of the product will be too high for you to make any money on a free-plus-shipping offer. For example, if your IPO costs you $30 a unit, you'll have a hard time making up that margin with your upsells. In this case, I recommend using a different kind of sales angle: a deep discount.

> **Item price can help you figure out whether to use a F+S or deep discount sales angle. For example, if your IPO will sell for less than about $10, I recommend using F+S. If your IPO is more than $10, try using deep discount.**

Deep discount offers are generally more profitable than free-plus-shipping ones. Look how our profit margins increase as the customer purchases more product.

But they do take a lot more testing and adjustments to get just right. If you do choose a deep discount offer and sales aren't coming through the funnel, remember that you proved your niche and your IPO, so the problem must be somewhere in your offer.

Design Your Sales Funnel

FUNNEL ECOSYSTEM & BUSINESS FUNDAMENTALS

PRODUCT IDEA	QUANTITY	COST + SHIPPING	SELL PRICE	PROFIT	SUPPLIER LINK	PRICE COMPARABLE?	NOTES
FLY-FISHING FLIES 1	X1	$3.66	$6.97	$3.31		YES	FRONT-END PRODUCT
FLY-FISHING FLIES 1	X2	$5.21	$8.97	$3.76		YES	
FLY-FISHING FLIES 1	X4	$8.31	$14.97	$6.66		YES	
FLY-FISHING FLIES 1	X6	$11.41	$21.97	$10.56		YES	
FLY-FISHING FLIES 1	X8	$14.51	$29.97	$15.46		YES	
FLY-FISHING STORAGE BOX	X1	$7.84	$14.97	$7.13		YES	ORDER BUMP

> **EMPIRE BUILDER EXERCISE**
>
> 1. Return to your list of possible IPOs.
>   - Does the one you've chosen still make sense?
>   - Does it lend itself to a free-plus-shipping or deep discount offer?
>   - Or does the IPO you've initially chosen work better as a complementary product?
> 2. From Amazon, type in keywords for your IPO. Look at the products under Most Wished For. Would any of those items work in your funnel?
> 3. Write down at least 10 different complementary products to prove.

Before taking a deep dive into each component of your funnel, I want to explain an overarching concept. When you start building out your funnel, your goal is to make the process as simple as possible for the customer. The real genius of a sales funnel is that it takes the customer through a predefined set of steps. The moment that path becomes convoluted or cumbersome, or they feel it wastes their time, they will leave your site. That's why you're going to make every step a binary yes or no choice.

- Will you opt in with your email address? Yes or no.
- Do you want more of this product for 20% less? Yes or no.
- Do you want to add in this order bump? Yes or no.

The moment you give them a third option, you've lost the sale.

Read on to learn more about how you will actually set up each section of your funnel.

OPT-IN/SALES PAGES

As you know by now, the opt-in is the first page of your funnel. You can play around with different features here, but generally, I like to include the following:

- Sales copy
- Images and/or video
- Reviews and testimonials
- Opt-in/sales page

Sales Copy

Sales copy refers to the words on the page that will help sell the product. Good sales copy needs to show the customer the result they can get with your product. Remember, you aren't necessarily selling a product so much as the desired outcome that your prospect wants. My fishing company doesn't just sell flies; it sells the chance to go fishing with your family or enjoy quiet time in nature.

I always think about this difference in reference to Popeye. Imagine that Popeye were a sales ad instead of a cartoon. If that were the case, he wouldn't be selling spinach, he'd be selling huge muscles. Yes, your sales page should include actual facts about the product, but it must also include the result that the prospect can achieve with the help of that product.

Sales angles are a major component of sales copy. Angles like scarcity (limited supply or limited time), money-back guarantees, warranties, or percent donated to a charity work well here.

For example, where the customer chooses the quantity of product, it might read "While supplies last," which incentivizes them to think about getting more. Or you could feature the charity you donate to somewhere on that page.

Images And Video

A great way to help your viewer see the result of the product is through quality images and video.

It's worth the investment to hire someone to produce great photos for you. On sites like Fiverr, you will find really competitive pricing. My business also offers this service. Check out EcommerceEmpireBuilders.com/services.

But make sure they aren't just generic photoshopped images or stock photos on white backgrounds. Remember, you want to show the customer the ideal results they can expect. If you sell dog chew toys, include images of puppies gnawing on them. If you're selling camping lights, show an image of two tents lit up in a national park.

Photos like these are commonly called lifestyle images, and including them on your sales page will dramatically improve your conversion and create more credibility around your brand.

Don't be afraid to take these photos yourself. (You can always have them professionally edited afterward.) When you receive your IPO during product testing, make sure to snap a few images with your smartphone.

If you ever need photos in a pinch, reach out to the supplier and ask for some. Usually they have a huge portfolio of images that they'll let you use.

Reviews And Testimonials

Reviews and testimonials are key for repeat business. When you first get started, you won't have any, so reach out to your supplier and ask for some reviews you can use. You can also give products away for free in return for testimonials, as I mentioned earlier.

Opt-in/Sales Page

I think about sales and opt-in pages as a single step in your funnel. The goal of the opt-in is to gather the prospect's email address.

Why would you want to make your customers go through the hassle of giving you an email address? For one, you want to follow up with them later. And two, because it's a way to validate the prospect. You see, not everyone who comes to your site is actually going to buy from you. And generally, if someone won't even give you their email address, you're not going to make the sale. Most importantly, as I'll prove to you later, your email list is the only asset you will truly own in your business. For now, just trust me on that.

I've found that about 40% of web traffic will opt in, with about 12% converting to sales.

Another option is a two-step order form where the opt-in is combined with the order form and order bump. This method minimizes your customer's effort even further by combining the opt-in/sales page and the order form and order bump into one easy page.

Usually the two-step order form has a conversion rate of about 10% because the lead is higher quality, given that they have already entered much of their personal information.

ORDER FORMS AND ORDER BUMPS

A standard order form is pretty simple. Here they will input their shipping and billing information and choose the number of units they'd like to purchase.

I like to include a few more elements here to establish credibility. I might restate the guarantee, put a link to our customer support, and show a few more positive reviews. Whatever you can do to make your customer feel comfortable is worth adding.

Another feature on this page is the order bump. This upsell is the equivalent to the pack of gum at a grocery store—it's inexpensive and something your customer is likely to want. Limited-edition items, carriers or cases for the item, e-books, digital products, warranties, and accessories make great order bumps.

Information products make great order bumps too. For example, if you sold paintbrushes, you might include a downloadable tutorial on how to select the best ones or how to clean and store them to ensure they last a long time as an order bump. These products do take some time to create and design, but you only need to create them once and they'll continue to benefit you for the life of your funnel.

If you're just starting out, you might not have any information products developed. Consider making something simple, like a one-page fact sheet or list of FAQs. You can also purchase and sell e-books in your niche that are already written.

Finally, you need some kind of payment gateway connected to this page. This would be a merchant service that authorizes credit card payment processing for e-businesses. Some of the most popular sites are PayPal and Stripe, but there are others.

After the customer purchases the product and says yes or no to the order bump, they'll land on the upsell page.

UPSELLS: DEEP DISCOUNT

The goal of your upsells is to increase the average cart value of each customer who buys from you. As you'll recall, your sequences of upsells will be a binary option, where the buyer can either choose each item or decline. Because the customer has already input their credit card information, you reduce their resistance to adding on more items and make it easier to do so.

Often the first upsell will be a deep discount. The buyer can either purchase the item or decline and continue to the next step of the funnel.

I usually offer two deep discounts directly after my order form purchase. The first will be four more units of the IPO at 20% off what they saw on the order form. Next they'll get an offer for an additional two units at 30% off.

The reason I told you earlier that your IPO should be something people will want to buy continuously is so that they'll be more likely to purchase your upsells that are multiples of the same product. If you sell a grill, it's unlikely you'll convince someone to buy four more. But if you sell flowerpots, you can probably sell five at a time.

That being said, the kinds of products customers will buy multiples of might surprise you.

One of my students is in the laser hair-removal niche, and their IPO is a handheld, battery-powered laser hair-removal tool. With that product you might think, *Why would anyone want more than one?* With some good marketing and a deep discount that customers can't refuse, my student has shown his customers that they need one in every room of the house and also as gifts for their friends and family members!

To be clear, you don't have to do a deep discount offer, and it certainly doesn't have to be the first upsell after the order form. This is just the sequence I've had the most success with. After two deep discount upsells, the customer moves to continuity.

UPSELLS: CONTINUITY

Continuity is essentially recurring revenue, and it's what is going to make you a ton of money in your funnel.

My wife taught me about this concept. At the time, she was my girlfriend and we were living in an old house. I was just getting started in my fishing business and trying to figure out how to make it profitable. We were really trying to save money at the time, so I was surprised when she brought in a box that had just been delivered.

I asked, "What's in the box?"

And she said, "Oh, it's makeup. It comes every month."

I was dumbfounded. What a brilliant sales angle! Why wasn't I doing something like this in my business?

There are a ton of subscription-based companies around. Like Bark Box, a business that sends monthly dog toys, and Dollar Shave Club, which mails out new razor blades every month. They are money-making machines.

Now you may have noticed a key difference between my fishing continuity subscription and that of a company like Bark Box or Dollar Shave Club: those companies offer a subscription as a front-end product rather than as a back-end upsell. This model can work, but I don't care for it for a few reasons.

The first is that they are just harder to sell. For example, your front-end product may convert at 15%, while your subscription service might convert at 2%. Why? Because it's a bigger obligation and it's more expensive. And when an offer is a greater commitment for the consumer, it's going to be more expensive to get them to buy it—meaning you'll spend more in advertising—and it's going to take more work to establish credibility.

In my fishing funnel, I actually tried to sell a subscription as a front-end offer in the beginning. And I had to wait six months before I could pay myself. People were signing up for it, but the average customer only stayed in the program for five or six months. (This holds true in the broader ecommerce industry.) Incidentally, it takes about that long before you start making money.

Why does it take so long? In part, because it's a big commitment for you. To get your customers interested, you often have to do a break-even offer where the first month or so is at cost (or even free). So not only will it take a while for you to make money, you'll also need a serious investment to get started, and that's without factoring in advertising.

A major reason other companies can go this route is because they are venture-backed, meaning they have received millions of dollars from investors. In those situations, entrepreneurs can handle waiting half a year to turn a profit or can afford break-even offers.

Again, you can place your upsells wherever you'd like to in your funnel. But when I test the sequence across multiple niches, I find that continuity as an upsell works best as the third step, especially if the first two are both deep discount offers. If a customer has already accepted two deep discount offers, they have already shown that they do not have much resistance to the sale.

When considering your upsell sequence, it's all about presenting whichever item they will have the least opposition to. That's why an order bump or a small, inexpensive item should go first. If someone is going to move through your funnel, this product is the one they are most likely to buy.

The same standard holds true for your discounted offers. If someone buys from your initial order form, they will likely say yes to an additional product at a better price. And if they've said yes to all three, the odds are good that they would appreciate a done-for-you subscription service that delivers products to their door.

So what makes a good continuity service? Read on for some key features of a great subscription program.

- **Consumable products:** Anything that can be consumed will work well as subscriptions because the customer will run out and need more later. For example, if you're in the cat training niche, perhaps you'll send monthly bags of training treats. If you are in the free-trade organic coffee bean niche, a biweekly bag of beans will always be in demand.

- **Easily lost or broken items:** Pet and children's toys are always breaking or becoming lost in couch cushions. And sporting equipment like tennis balls and golf balls are perpetually lost to the outdoors.
- **Single-use products:** Some products are only designed to be used once, and therefore will need to be repurchased each time. Think about items like stickers, disposable plates, and hand warmers. Customers may even want to stock up in bulk for some items.
- **Items that need to be refilled or replaced:** Many hobbies involve products that periodically need to be refilled or replaced. For an artist, think watercolor paints, fine art brushes, and coloring pads. For a woodworker, think sandpaper and sealers.
- **Collectibles:** One popular subscription service is a "t-shirt of the month club." So if you're in the gaming market, every month you could send your customers a cool t-shirt with a new design relating to the latest games.
- **Information products:** E-books, FAQs, fact sheets, and how-to videos are great subscription services. For example, someone in the body-building niche could offer a recurring monthly payment for access to their beach-body-on-demand program, or a video game niche could offer weekly game recommendations.

  One of the superpowers of an information product, particularly as a continuity piece, is that you don't have to deal with shipping.
- **Group access:** A friend of mine is a great chef in the grilling niche. He offers a subscription service that gives his customers access to his Facebook group, where he goes

live every week. Thousands of people pay $9.99 a month to just watch him smoke meat.

Don't be afraid to get creative! Another easy subscription service is a product testers club, where members gain early access to items you might sell in the future.

For any subscription program, you'll want to do some testing to see whether your offer should be a monthly or yearly plan.

> **EMPIRE BUILDER EXERCISE**
>
> How can you build continuity into your funnel? Write down at least one idea in each category below.
>
> - Consumable
> - Easily lost or broken
> - Collectible
> - Information product
> - Group access
>
> Which of these ideas get you most excited?
>
> Remember there are pros and cons to each. For example, if you offer a physical product, you will have to make sure that it is shipped monthly and on time. If it is a collectible, you might have to come up with a new design every month. An information product takes a lot of effort to create on the front end, while group access takes a while to build up a community and requires monthly, weekly, or even daily attention.

What kind of subscription service will work best in your niche?

A critical component of continuity is a subscribe-and-save element. People are more likely to sign up for your service if they are incentivized by a good deal. Amazon has made this extremely popular. Through their Subscribe & Save service, you can have paper towels delivered to your door for 2% less than you would pay if you just bought them once or one at a time.

If you plan to send physical products in the mail, you should charge double the product cost. Any subscription should be at a 50% margin.

Pricing information products or group access is a little trickier. You have to try to determine the value of the information being given, while taking into consideration how much your customers will be willing to spend. What is the result they will achieve worth to them in dollars? This is a good time to check in with your competition. What are they charging for similar services?

Also, how can you increase the perceived value of your product? The answer to this question applies to any kind of continuity piece. Your monthly membership must sound cool and exclusive. You want your members to feel like they're part of a community that will improve their lives in some critical way.

A subscribe-and-save model can be a decent starting point. However, continuing to add value will really keep people around longer. And ideally you want them to be engaged for years. To do that, you have to create a real following around whatever you're selling.

For example, Dollar Shave Club doesn't just send you a razor, they also send a bathroom reader, a little comic-style book with fun facts and stories to read in the bathroom. It's funny and cool, and makes you feel like you're a part of an exclusive club. Heck, they even baked the word *club* into their brand name.

You're not just offering monthly discounted products; you're offering them an exclusive opportunity to be in the Barbecue Smoker's Association or the Small Puppy Society or Fly Fishing United. You are offering them a community of people with shared interests.

It sure sounds like a ton of work to create this community, doesn't it? Frankly, you're right. You probably don't have time to focus that many hours on your continuity piece when you are just trying to get your funnel up and running. And that's why you might instead create a product testers club.

The *[Insert Your Niche Here]* Testers Club will give your customers access to new items from your supplier every single month. One thing that's great about this community is that they won't expect much from you aside from a discount on cool new products, which means you'll have plenty of time to focus on the rest of your funnel. More importantly, this club is going to help you prove new products as well.

I like to position this group as an opportunity to try out the latest trends in the industry. And you will be able to deliver on that promise, because as you start looking through your supplier catalogue, you'll see new products come through all the time. Your customers can test them out and give feedback inside a private Facebook group or on your website.

You might find that access to a group and a subscribe-and-save offer isn't enough to get folks into your continuity piece. But don't be tempted to give up. Continuity will ultimately be one of the most profitable elements of your business. Sure there is some fluctuation, but it is generally more stable than other offer types.

In fact, in my own business, my continuity pieces alone pay my salary, while profits from the rest of the funnels are reinvested into my company.

So if people aren't biting, what can you do? Try offering free or inexpensive trials. They might pay half price for six months or $1 for a 30-day trial. You could also give away a free bonus item just for agreeing to participate in the trial.

If you do a trial, especially if you package it with another offer, make sure you include the total value. For example, if I were to offer a $7 trial for the first seven days of Fly Fishing United plus a free set of 10 flies, I'd calculate the total value of this package at $19.97. So for $7, the customer receives $20 in overall value.

Another great trial offer is a break-even deal. So if it costs you $10 to buy and deliver the product, the customer will only pay $10 during the trial period.

So back to the funnel process. After your customer opts in to your subscription service, you can either take them to a thank-you page (if you have a shorter funnel) or to your complementary products.

UPSELLS: COMPLEMENTARY PRODUCTS

Upsells #4 and #5 are often more expensive complementary products within your niche. At first, you might not want to offer any more upsells after the continuity piece, and that's fine. The more products you sell, the more complicated your business becomes. But eventually, you may want to add them. And digital products make excellent upsells, as you only have to create them once and can then sell for 100% margin.

Again, if you're looking for inspiration, type your IPO's keywords into Amazon and check out the "Frequently bought together" and Most Wished For items. If you're just getting started, upsells #4 and #5 are really just a place for you to try out a few other products to see if they work in your niche.

Finally, the customer comes to the last page of your funnel.

THANK-YOU PAGE

You might think there's nothing to talk about in this section. After all, how complicated can a simple thank-you be? You're right… to an extent. On this page, obviously you'll want to include information like…

- Text that reads "Thank you for your purchase" or something similar
- Contact details for customer support
- Links to your social media channels

You'll also want to have specs on the deliverables they just bought, like…

- Estimated delivery time/date
- Product image
- More product reviews

But wait—there's more!

If someone has moved all the way through your funnel, they might be ready to purchase more, or at least check out what else you have to offer. This makes this final page the perfect opportunity to send them to your other funnels.

Include clickable images of your other IPOs under text that reads "You might also like" or something similar. For example, if they just went through a funnel for home workout equipment, they might see an image for a healthy meals cookbook or a meal plan subscription. Drive that traffic to your other channels while they are still in a buying mood!

Right now, you probably don't have any other funnels, but that doesn't mean you can't make money on your thank-you page. For example, you could insert affiliate links. An affiliate is a company that will pay you a commission on any sales you drive to their site. One of the easiest ways to start offering affiliate products is through Amazon. What products do they sell that are complementary to yours? Or maybe you can dig into your indirect competition file and agree to send traffic to each other's funnels.

If you're short on time, consider using the affiliate marketplace ClickBank or Amazon Associates, where you can simply plug products in and have it set up in just a few minutes.

Don't forget to mention your Facebook group on this page as well. You'll soon learn that this is an asset to your business, therefore you always want to invest time and effort in your social media presence. Some ecommerce folks just want to make front-end sales and never talk to their customers again. But those people don't make much money, and I want you to be as profitable as you can be.

And always remember, just because you're done selling doesn't mean someone is done buying. That's why it's so critical to continue to sell on your thank-you page.

Trends, companies, and software come and go. But I am quite sure the basic sales funnel is here to stay. With its ability to replicate the experience of a face-to-face transaction with a salesperson, this method of selling products has revolutionized ecommerce. The specific platform you use to generate your funnel may change over time. But regardless of which one you choose, the basic principles will stay the same.

(For the latest news and trends, keep your eye on the Ecommerce Empire Builders YouTube channel and podcast).

WATCHING YOUR METRICS

Once you build your funnel, you should watch your metrics like it's your day job (and it kind of is). If your upsells aren't converting, change them out. If your order bump isn't getting any sales, consider a different offer.

You need to be obsessed with your numbers. Track everything, including total sales, cost of goods sold, and total profit. You should know how many opt-ins you have in a day, what your conversion rate is, and how many sales go through on your order forms.

Once your funnel is up and running, you'll be wondering when to start making adjustments to your price. I have a magic number for my students: 1.6.

That is, when your units sold divided by the total number of customers is greater than 1.6, it's time to raise your price.

ADJUSTING YOUR PRICE

MAGIC NUMBER: 1.6

$$\frac{\text{UNITS SOLD}}{\text{CUSTOMERS}} = \frac{1,925}{500} = {}^*3.85$$

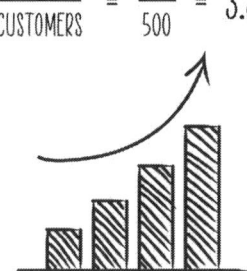

500 ORDERS:

11% - 55 ORDERS (55 UNITS) - $218.35
24% - 120 ORDERS (240 UNITS) - $956.40
38% - 190 ORDERS (760 UNITS) - $2,844.30
21% - 105 ORDERS (630 UNITS) - $2,306.85
6% - 30 ORDERS (240 UNITS) - $899.10

TOTAL: $7,225.00
TOTAL UNITS = 1,925

GREATER THAN 1.6? RAISE THE PRICE!

There could also be times when you need to lower your price. Maybe no one is biting on your offer, so you'd like to narrow the margins on a loss leader to entice more prospects to buy. In this case, I recommend lowering your price if the number of units sold divided by total customers is *less than* 1.6.

There is of course some wiggle room here, and you'll want to play around with your margins. However, 1.6 has been an effective benchmark for my ecommerce business.

Typically, I suggest shooting for a 20% margin on the front-end offer.

Another way to think about price lowering is that if you are less than the magic number, you know that customers just aren't buying enough volume. Many people think that if their margins are low, they just need more customers. That isn't always the case. Instead, it's more an indication that you need to either pick an IPO that people will want multiples of or choose complementary products that people will want to buy in bulk.

On the flip side, don't break something that's already working. If you're hitting that magic number of 1.6, leave your funnel alone. If it's not converting, consider building a new funnel around a different IPO with different upsells.

A word of advice: Don't make any changes to your funnel without data to back up that decision. So many people fall for this mistake. They will just start tinkering with their funnel without understanding why (or whether) those changes might make a difference. Always let the data tell you what to do.

FUNNEL #1	25 SALES PER DAY X $30 AVERAGE CART = $750
FUNNEL #2	25 SALES PER DAY X $30 AVERAGE CART = $750
FUNNEL #3	25 SALES PER DAY X $30 AVERAGE CART = $750
FUNNEL #4	25 SALES PER DAY X $30 AVERAGE CART = $750

Your goal should be to average about 25 sales a day in your funnel. You might not get there right away, but it's a great starting point. Once you hit that, you can go and build out your next one and your next one, and eventually you'll hit your seven-figure goal.

Speaking of that goal…let's revisit it.

A single funnel, despite being extremely profitable, might not get you to seven figures. That's why you'll likely need to build out at least three additional funnels.

In the example below, each funnel represents a different product.

In this model, you're doing $3,000 in revenue per day.

$750 x 4 = $3,000

If those daily sales hold steady, you can surpass one million within one year.

$3,000 x 365 = $1,095,000

Can you believe it's possible to hit seven figures without selling hundreds of products?

One final note: Before you start driving traffic to your first funnel, you should verify that everything is working correctly. To do so, change all the product prices to $1 and purchase each one as a test. Fix any bugs along the way, and make sure your products arrive on time and in good shape.

By this point, you have identified your market, your niche, and an IPO. You've contacted some suppliers and identified some possible upsells. You're immersed in your niche by joining various groups and studying your competitors. You know the influencers in your space and you know who is buying which product. You've combined all that knowledge to produce a funnel.

Now you just have to find some customers.

CHAPTER 7

DRIVE TRAFFIC TO YOUR FUNNEL

I have a question for you, and it might make you squirm a little. But you've agreed to get comfortable with being uncomfortable, so stick with me here.

Why should your customers buy from you?

They've never seen you or your business before.

They've never even heard of you.

Why would they give you their payment information?

Before you respond, I have another question for you.

When was the last time you bought something from a Facebook advertisement? My clients often respond, "Oh, I've never done that." Yet we expect our customers to buy from us anyway. How can we ensure that others will do something we rarely do ourselves? We have to combat that skepticism.

Your irresistible offer is one way you'll entice them. At the very least, it will give you a strong advantage over any competitor.

But for a lot of your potential buyers, a good deal just won't be enough.

There are three foundational points to selling anything to anyone.

- Credibility
- Emotion
- Logic

You are going to use these factors in every advertisement, email, and funnel you create to ensure that your customers trust you with their credit cards. Let's explore each of these in more detail.

Credibility

As a new Ecommerce Empire Builder, you have a huge challenge ahead of you: to establish credibility in a space where no one has ever heard of you. That is extremely difficult to do. But there are a few ways to go about it.

- **Try offering a money-back guarantee.** This is a great way to make buyers feel safe and secure in the case that the product arrives broken or damaged. Also, this kind of guarantee signals that you stand by your product and your business. Product scams don't offer guarantees. But make sure you include a reasonable time limit on this offer; otherwise, anyone could request a replacement at any time. A common time limit is 30 days.
- **Post product reviews and customer testimonials.** Eventually, you'll have lots of glowing reviews from influencers and happy customers. But at first you won't have any. What to do?

You're going to have to get a little resourceful. Ask the supplier you are drop-shipping from for reviews. Show your customers that your product has a five-star rating and that 7,000 people have already purchased it.

- **Establish credibility with images of the product being used.** Don't rely on a classic stock photo of your product with a white background. Instead, include photos of the product getting the desired result for the customer.

A private client of mine sold a remote control race car. He asked me to diagnose any problems with his funnel. I noticed that he had lots of great photos of the product. However, there was something missing. When I landed on the home page, there was no image showing me what the product did or who it was for. It wasn't even clear that this race car was intended for children. So I told him to include a photo of a child using the product in his funnel.

Guess what? This one small tweak bumped his conversion rate from 3% to 10%!

Some of the best funnels I created for my fishing business relied on pictures of customers holding the fish they had caught. In that image, the customer can see that other people are getting the results they want. Also, quality photography in your funnel signals to buyers that you are legit. You can purchase professional photography services or even have another company do it for you. (Like ours at EcommerceEmpireBuilders.com/services.)

Or you can take your own photos. When you purchase a product for testing, snap a few photos. With some decent lighting and a smartphone, you can capture some good imagery. I took the products to the lake near my home and snapped pictures of the lures on some rocks and in the water. Trust me, an image of the product actually being used as intended will do so much more for you than a generic photo.

- **Offer customer service support.** You can do this by including your customer support phone number and email on the order forms. This will help the customer feel safer, knowing there is someone who can respond to any problems, questions, or issues they might have. Of course, make sure you have a system in place to respond to calls and emails promptly.

  A live chat feature on your site is also helpful. You can set one up using a sales-funnel software, but you can also easily create one on your Facebook business page. Even if no one ever actually uses it, the fact that it's there adds credibility to your business.

- **Include a variety of features.** A feature could be a BuzzFeed article, a shoutout on a YouTube channel, or a blog post. It will take time to have your product featured, and it isn't completely necessary, but it does prove to your customers that you are a legit company.

One way to get featured is to send your IPO to a product review website or forum. There are lots of these sites across various niches, testing out running shoes and cooking equipment and keyboards and paint and whatever else you could possibly imagine. A favorable review will go a long way for your business and drive traffic to your site.

Emotion

Credibility isn't enough on its own to sell anything to anyone. Ideally, you want your prospect to have an emotional experience with your product. And you can create that connection by showing the incredible results that other customers have achieved. Images of your customers using the product and getting results from it will help them have an emotional response to what you are selling. As I mentioned, I love using images of our customers and our reviews on AliExpress and Amazon.

Nobody buys a drill because they just want to own a drill. They want what the tool can do. They want to drill a hole in their wall so they can hang up pictures of their family, so they can turn the basement into a game room for the kids, or maybe so their friends think they are the kind of person who is really handy.

Creating emotion is all about selling results. It's about showing a fisherman (or woman) they can catch a bigger, better carp or bass. It's proving to someone that they really can lose 10 more pounds. It's convincing someone that your protein powder can help them bulk up or that your training program can help reduce muscle cramping.

You may have heard the expression "People buy based on emotion and justify the purchase with logic." Consider watches. You can easily spend $10K on a fancy watch or you can buy one for $5 on Amazon. And guess what? They'll do the exact same thing: tell time.

But some people want the expensive watch because of the emotional connection they have with it. It's sleek and it has a beautiful design. It suggests power and confidence. It's something to collect. They might also justify the purchase logically, but you can bet they bought it primarily based on emotion.

Logic

So if everyone buys based on emotion, why would I bother adding in any logic? For one thing, you don't want to make your customers work hard to justify buying your product. Sure, they might want to buy a box of your neon shoestrings because they think their kids would like them, but you can help them overcome resistance to that sale if you also show them what a good deal it is.

And some people really do want to know all the details. For those folks, make sure you include information like product weight, dimensions, materials used, and whether assembly is required. Showing that you are extremely familiar with your product also further establishes credibility.

But these people don't just want to hear about the details; they also want a justification for buying the product. To establish that, you could show them how your product is a better deal than your competitor's, or how it's made with higher-quality materials. Perhaps it's sourced in the US instead of overseas.

The idea is that your customers are looking for a reason to feel good about the purchase, and you are going to give it to them. Check out some articles that discuss the benefits of your product. For my supplement, I found articles from credible sites talking about the properties of all the ingredients. You can use that material to help write your own copy. Make sure you always credit the original source though.

Here's an example of how you might use credibility, emotion, and logic to sell a product.

Imagine you sell matches to outdoor enthusiasts. You might say something like…

"Survival matches are long-lasting, waterproof, and easy to use. They burn at over 600 degrees Fahrenheit, and each match has the capacity of 50,000 regular matches."

The ad gives all the relevant info, including numbers and figures that suggest what it is capable of, while creating an emotional connection with the word "survival." How many people do you think actually need a waterproof match that burns at 600 degrees? Not many. But they buy it because of how it makes them feel—like a survivalist.

Next they might say something like, "We offer 100% satisfaction with a money-back guarantee." Remember, a guarantee is a great way to establish credibility, showing that you truly stand by your product.

If you sold earrings, you might want to tell your customer that they look great whether your hair is up or down. Maybe you mention that they won't get caught in curly hair. You'll include details like "Crafted with care, they are 10 millimeters long and nickel-free." And of course, you'd add: "We offer a full refund if you don't love this product."

Every time you write sales copy, consider how you can work credibility, emotion, and logic into your pitch.

EMPIRE BUILDER EXERCISE

Make a plan for how you will establish credibility, emotion, and logic within your funnel. Refer to the lingo you included in the Niche Research folder, and include any special keywords or phrases that will assure your customers that you understand them and your niche. Make sure to snag some reviews or find some articles talking about the benefits of your product.

UNDERSTANDING TRAFFIC

In terms of sales, traffic refers to the number of users who visit a website. There are essentially three types of customer traffic out there: cold, warm, and hot.

- **Cold traffic** is made up of people who have never heard of you before. They don't know your brand and they don't know what you sell.
- **Warm traffic** includes people who are somewhat familiar with you but haven't bought anything from you yet. For example, if an influencer promotes your product to their audience, they've just turned them into warm traffic. Because their followers know and trust them, they will be warmed up to the sale. This also includes anyone who follows you on social media.
- **Hot traffic** refers to people who have already bought from you, so they are most likely to know, like, and trust you and therefore buy more.

So why do you care where people are coming from? Does it really matter, as long as they find your funnel? Who cares whether they come from a Facebook advertisement or an influencer? Does it make a difference whether they come from a blog or a YouTube video? The short answer is yes, and that's because the warmer the traffic, the better the conversion.

You can also think about traffic in the context of control. Within this schema, there are four different types.

- Traffic you **own**
- Traffic you **earn**

- Traffic you **control**
- Traffic that you **do not** control

You'll vary your marketing approach depending on these different categories.

Traffic You Own

You can think of owned traffic as your assets. One of the biggest assets in this category is your email list. And I know what you're saying: "Does anyone buy from email reminders anymore?"

Yes! They absolutely do, and I believe they will continue to do so.

But there is another reason that an email list is essential. It is one of the few assets that you own 100%, and therefore control 100%. It is something you can download to a USB drive and carry around in your pocket.

Remember when I completely lost my customer base with the FBA business? Without an email list, you could find yourself in a similar position. Amazon, Shopify, and Etsy customers can disappear overnight. Facebook groups can be shut down, Instagram accounts deleted, and YouTube channels closed.

And if you think that's uncommon, think again. I know lots of people who lost their business overnight to Amazon's own branded products. When the company sees a popular product, they'll just offer their own version. And you can guess which product they'll recommend first.

I think of an email list as an insurance policy. No matter what happens to my business, I will *never* have to start over from scratch again.

If you're brand new to ecommerce, you probably don't own any traffic. That's okay, because the funnel you'll create will generate it for you.

Traffic You Control

Traffic you control comes in three flavors.

- **Paid advertising:** Consider Facebook Ads or Google Ads as traffic you control. You put money into the machine, and it turns out customers.
- **Paid influencers:** When you start reaching out to influencers in your niche, many of them will be willing to promote your product for a fee.
- **Affiliates:** These are people who promote your products in exchange for a commission. They might put a link to your product in one of their blog posts or under a YouTube video. Every time someone clicks on the link and purchases the product, the affiliate gets a commission.

Traffic That You Earn

This is all about business relationships with people who have the eyeballs of your target niche. While this could be an influencer, that isn't always the case.

For example, I could ask a YouTuber to promote my product. And they could respond, "Sure…for five thousand dollars." But you might not have $5,000 to hand to someone you don't know. It may very well be a good investment, but you are building a low-cost, low-risk business and therefore won't be making investments like that (yet).

If you've decided that you absolutely must work with this influencer, you're going to have to take the time to build up a relationship. Send them some of your products for free and begin promoting their channel on your platforms. Spend plenty of time engaging with them and offering value without asking for anything in return.

Traffic You Don't Control

With this traffic, you may have no idea how it got to your funnel, but somehow it did. Perhaps this person found you on Google or someone posted your product in their Facebook feed. Maybe they found out about you from word of mouth. And because you don't know where these buyers are coming from, it's even *more* essential to capture their email right away.

Before you can get this traffic, it's vital to set up your social media presence.

Social Media

Because you're immersed in your niche, you already know which social media platforms your future customers are hanging out on. So it makes sense to maintain a social media presence there.

Some entrepreneurs feel uncomfortable or daunted by the task of maintaining social media accounts. They feel like their business isn't big enough or they are stressed over the idea of posting new content. They may feel insecure and vulnerable when they consider the stress and implications of putting their fledgling business out into the world. For many, one of the biggest challenges is overcoming fear of rejection on a public platform.

But please don't let your emotions get in the way of your success. Remember, the New You is getting comfortable being uncomfortable.

Your success on social media depends on two things: frequency and consistency. Your posts don't have to be perfect, but you should be putting up new stuff on a regular basis.

You'll often hear successful entrepreneurs say that if you can post daily for 365 days, at the end of the year, you will be financially free. While it does take more than a social media presence to grow a business, they are right in saying that daily postings can be huge for your success.

So let's set up your social media engine. I call it this because it's something you only have to put effort into once, then it runs by itself for an entire week or month.

The first thing you'll need is a **profile**. When setting up a profile, don't write a long-winded story about who you are and why you started your business. For one thing, no one would probably read it. And at this point, they don't really care. You're not popular, credible, or relevant (yet).

Instead, write something short and to the point. Often the platform itself will help you with this by setting limits on how many characters can be used. Use the max amount of space that the platform will allow. And most importantly, include a link to your funnel.

Your first post should be your company logo. You can hire someone on a site like Fiverr to create this graphic.

Next, write a post that explains who you are and why your company exists. Make sure your support email is clearly visible. No matter the platform, your profile has to exude credibility. Why? Because buyers want to feel that they're in a risk-free environment and that it's a no-brainer to do business with you.

Part of finding followers includes proper tagging on social sites and placing relevant hashtags on your posts. This allows people who are in your niche to find you. But to be sure, growth will be slow in the beginning. No one wants to follow you when you're at zero, making it imperative to get friends and family involved.

Although you should post frequently and consistently, you don't have to do it every single day. Instead, choose a time during the week when you're feeling creative, and schedule your posts out a week to a month in advance.

You're likely saying, "That's all fine, Pete, but what am I going to post about every day?"

Some of your content you'll create yourself and some of it you'll repost from other people. For your own content, post lifestyle photos that show the benefits of the product. What will the customer achieve if they buy it?

On platforms like Facebook, you can share blog articles, videos, and any other kind of long-form content. You can also repost stuff that your followers created. And as long as you give proper credit, you can share other people's images as well.

This strategy works really well on platforms like Instagram. Look for popular hashtags in your niche and repost images that people like. Is there an influencer in your niche who everyone loves? Share their content and, in the caption, give credit and explain why you like what they've created.

You can also pay influencers to create posts for you. Send them the product for free and they might even do it without payment.

EMPIRE BUILDER EXERCISE

1. Find out which social media sites your ideal customers hang out on.
2. Check out your competitors' social profiles. Note the kind of images and hashtags they use and how often they post. Read their bios. You can use this information to help build out your own profile.
3. Create or update your profile for each social media site you'll use to market your funnel.
4. Create a schedule for the next week noting when you will post to each platform and the topics you will use. There are plenty of social media management tools out there to help automate this process.

Notes

Posting Schedule

Day 1

Day 2

Day 3

Day 4

Day 5

Day 6

Day 7

At this point, you have a profile on each of your social sites. You also have a link to an operating funnel, and you've scheduled out your content for the next week. So how do you get followers?

Friends And Family

This may seem obvious, but you'd be surprised by how few people are willing to reach out to their friends and family. It doesn't take much more than an email or social post that says, "Hey, I'm starting a new business. Would you follow my page?" This is the easiest way to get your first 100 or so followers. After contacting your friends and family, you can reach out to influencers.

Influencers

When people think of influencers, they generally think of Instagram. But an influencer can be on any platform—they are just someone who has a decent following in your niche. They might own a big email list, several YouTube channels, popular blogs, Reddit groups, or Facebook groups.

If you're just starting out, don't go directly to influencers who have a massive following (anything over 500,000 is probably too ambitious). While these people might have a greater reach than someone with a smaller fan base, they will also be quite expensive. More importantly, a person with that huge of a following generally isn't as laser-targeted in their niche. Instead, look for an influencer who targets the exact same niche as you and has about 10,000 followers.

If you're launching a funnel and have a tight budget, I recommend allocating between $250 and $500 to influencer marketing. Now you might be able to get influencer shoutouts just by sending them stuff for free. But generally, these influencers have a smaller following and therefore provide a smaller reach for your audience. I try to pay anywhere from $30 to $60 per shoutout or post. If they only offer a meme or image, I'll pay less.

Paying for an expensive influencer might not be in the budget for you right now. But you can use smaller ones (who have around 1,000 followers) to help promote your product and drive traffic to your social media. Try sending some influencers your product for free and you can bet they'll give you a shoutout at no cost. Most people love getting free swag! And chances are the product costs you less than what you would spend to create an ad.

If you have the capital, you can even tell these influencers you are doing a free giveaway on your social media account. Offer their followers a chance to win some of your products, and you might just get a percentage of these people to follow you as well.

Paid Ads

To run a profitable ad, you must understand how these platforms work. I couldn't possibly teach you how to make an ad for every platform out there in this book. And even if I did, the process would likely change by the time you read about it. So instead, I'll focus on strategy versus specific tactics.

All ad platforms have something called a **pixel id**. It's a piece of code installed on your funnel to track site engagement. If you've ever wondered why you're bombarded with ads after visiting a particular site, this is the pixel id working its magic.

The pixel is really the cornerstone to making advertising work for you, because it's what will allow you to track your metrics. With this code, you can see whether someone viewed your sales page or your order form. You can also find out if they gave you their email address or bought any of your upsells.

Another useful feature is **custom audiences**. This is essentially a way of grouping people together. I think about it as a series of different buckets. In one bucket is a group that gave you an email address but didn't make a sale. In another are all the folks who bought your IPO but didn't bite on your continuity product. Advertising platforms can group these people together for you.

Why would you want separate buckets? Because different buyers need to be reengaged in different ways. The practice of grouping your prospects and then engaging them to buy more products is called **retargeting**. Essentially, this is the practice of following up with that warm traffic—people who have shown interest in your products through ads, emails, and other marketing content—to get them back into the funnel.

For example, if you were an online bookseller and someone gave you their email address but didn't buy, you'll want to follow up by sending them an email reminding them about how awesome the new werewolf and vampire novel that they looked at recently is, with a link back to your order form. Those who did buy but didn't go for your subscription might need to see some complementary products, perhaps a silver bullet charm or branded bookmarks, to be convinced that they need to belong to your Book of the Month Club.

If retargeting sounds like a lot of work, remember this fundamental rule of marketing: the warmer the traffic, the easier the conversion. A person who gave you their email address is much more likely to buy from you than someone who has never heard of your brand. Likewise, someone who bought your IPO is much more likely to sign up for your subscription service if you present the offer again. Perhaps they just need to see more social proof or credibility, so you'll retarget them by emailing testimonials and reviews from existing customers.

Advertising platforms can retarget by showing your product advertisement in someone's feed. Imagine a potential customer visited your site but then left for whatever reason. Maybe they had something more important to do or they just didn't want your product right then and there.

But then the next time they are on that site, they see your ad. Some of those people will say, "Oh right—I forgot I wanted to buy that." At the very least, they might return to your site to learn more about your products. The more times they engage with you—via an ad, a follow-up email, or a return visit to your site—the more likely they are to buy from you one or more times. And once they become a loyal customer, they will also spread the word to their friends and family—free bonus marketing!

One feature of advertising platforms that you'll want to use is called **lookalike audiences**. These are a way to reach new people who are likely to be interested in your business because they're similar to your existing customers. How they do this is somewhat complicated, but actually using the program is quite simple.

Essentially, you choose a source audience, or a group created with information pulled from your pixel or fans of your page. The platform's algorithm will then identify the common qualities—for example, demographic information or interests—of the people who are already engaged with your brand. The platform then digitally crawls across its giant user database and finds all the people who fit the description of your ideal customer. They can find you hundreds or thousands of people who are like those in your group.

The best part is that the more data you give these advertising platforms, the better your results will be. The bad news is that these algorithms aren't especially useful until you have a large following. But once you've gained a few hundred customers through influencer traffic, you can start putting them to work.

Emails

Some say that email marketing is dead. But it's really not, and by now I hope I've convinced you of this.

Your email list is your #1 biggest asset for your business. In my opinion, it is truly the only tangible thing you have in your company.

In fact, it's so valuable that the number of contacts in your email list should equate to monthly revenue. So if you have 1,000 people on your email list, you should be making at least $1,000 per month. How? Through daily email broadcasts, which are individual emails you send to a group of subscribers in your contact list who are already warmed up to your business.

Abandoned cart emails, testimonials, and new offers are all possible with your email list. If someone comes to your funnel and doesn't buy, you can send them testimonials. If someone adds something to their cart but doesn't give their credit card info, you can send out an abandoned cart email. Or if you build out a new funnel, you can test it first on your email list to see if you get traction.

There are four lists I recommend you use.

- Welcome Series
- Buyers
- Continuity Buyers
- Master Bucket

Welcome Series List

The welcome series is a group of automated emails you send from your autoresponder to your subscribers so they can learn about your business. So as new people opt in by providing their email address, they will be sent a series of emails over a five-day period that allow them to get to know you a little better.

The ultimate goal of the welcome series is to ensure the customer feels comfortable enough to buy from you. This content might include an explanation of what your product is and how it benefits your customers, a series of videos on how people typically use your product, or your brand origin story—why you started your business in the first place.

Buyers List

The buyers list includes all the people who have bought at least one item from you. It's key to keep this list separate because these folks are more likely to buy from you again than cold or warm traffic. They already like and trust you, so they're going to be a much easier sell than trying to convert somebody who has never given you a dollar before.

Continuity Buyers List

This is a list of all the members who have joined your continuity program. I like to email these folks about specific things happening in the monthly subscription box. So for example, let's say we're sending out a new sloth mug to our customers in the next monthly Sloth Lovers box. I might allow this bucket early access to the product or even just send them a reminder to check it out and give us feedback on how they liked it in our Sloth Lovers of the World Facebook group.

Master Bucket List

The Master Bucket list is a default group that includes all of your subscribers. In this list, the emails sent could be about anything at all. It's just a chance to check in and keep your products and business top-of-mind.

I love this list because all roads lead to it. For example, once the customer comes through a welcome series, they'll transfer to the Master Bucket list, where they will get promotions and new offers.

You now have the tools you need to start a seven-figure funnel. You've chosen a niche you love and an initial product offering. You've built that IPO into a truly unbeatable offer filled with credibility, emotion, and logic. You've even created a money-making machine filled with upsells like deep discounts, order bumps, continuity, and complementary products.

At least, you've done all that in your head. Are you ready to make it happen?

CHAPTER 8

MANAGE YOUR WORKFLOW

A lot of people aspire to be entrepreneurs, but as you've seen, so many will fail. Why? Because time is our most valuable resource. You will never be able to get more of it, so you must protect it. To do that, you must have a strict routine and plan that you follow every single day. Once you become an entrepreneur, no one else is going to be watching out for you, looking over your shoulder to make sure you are doing what you need to.

While there are many ways to maximize workflow and productivity, I developed my own method to help structure my day (and yours) for maximum wellness and success. It's called the BUILD system. Each letter corresponds to a different daily goal. Here's how it works.

BODY

The first goal in BUILD is related to the body. You don't have to be healthy to be an entrepreneur, but it definitely gives you more energy, stamina, and mental capacity. And as you know, I believe in a business-integrated lifestyle. That means that you can't be successful in one area (ecommerce) without being successful in others.

You

The you (U) goal is fun and personal. Maybe you want to learn how to play chess or meditate or try out yoga. Whatever it is, this goal should be really enjoyable for you.

Income

Your income goal should increase your business profits. It's an activity that will positively impact your income today and/or in the future. It can be related to your business or a personal investment.

Relationships

A relationship goal can be personal or work-related. What relationship can you strengthen each day? Maybe plan a date night with your significant other or play a game with your kids.

Development

This one is all about learning new skills. Examples of these activities include reading a book, attending a training session, or listening to a podcast. What new, exciting topic do you want to learn about?

You will set new BUILD goals every quarter, so four times a year. I have a journal dedicated to documenting these goals along with my progress. Here are my BUILD goals from this quarter.

> **B: I will work out for 45 minutes.**
>
> **U: I will play chess for 30 minutes.**
>
> **I: I will reach out to 10 influencers in my niche.**
>
> **L: I will dedicate two uninterrupted hours to spend time with my family.**
>
> **D: I will watch one hour of training.**

If you choose to use this method, every day you'll write the word "BUILD" at the top of your journal. Once you achieve a goal, you'll circle it. If you miss one, cross it out with an X. If you hit all five, you've just had a five-point day! It should be hard to reach that goal. If you hit five points every day, you aren't stretching far enough. Your goals should push you.

The BUILD system can change your life. But it requires discipline. And that's why so many people don't stick with it. But I know you aren't going to take the easy way out, because you understand the power of compound interest.

What do I mean by that? Well if you followed my own personal BUILD plan, in three months you would have…

B > Worked out for 4,050 minutes

U > Played chess for 2,700 minutes

I > Reached out to 900 influencers

L > Spent 180 extra hours with someone you love

D > Completed 90 hours of personal development

And that's just a single quarter in a year. Think about the person you'll be in three months. That is who will create an Ecommerce Empire. So let's get you there.

EMPIRE BUILDER EXERCISE

Create a quarterly goal for each letter of BUILD.

B

U

I

L

D

Now post these somewhere visible and schedule a time each day to review them.

DAILY 6 & PTT

To go with the BUILD system, I use what I call a Daily 6 and Plan Tomorrow Today (PTT).

Now I know you're busy. But I'm sure you have an hour or two somewhere in your day to make this happen. And believe me, this is the only way it will.

Always remember, now that you're an entrepreneur, you will only get out of your business what you put into it. No one is going to make sure you reach your goals but you. And that's why you need to stay accountable to yourself—to make a *promise* to yourself—every single day. You're going to do that with a Daily 6 and PTT.

Your Daily 6 consists of the six tasks you promise yourself you'll do today that will move your business forward. Notice that it's not 100, it's not 50, it's not even 20. To make this sustainable, you must be realistic about what you can achieve in a day. And you will need to focus completely.

Each task should have an allotted amount of time, enough to do the task well. Give yourself permission to do things right.

PTT means that tasks are planned the night before and thought through properly. Your days of waking up and not knowing where to begin are over. That's the habit of someone who doesn't control their time, and you're not that person.

This is the last task I do each day before I spend time with my family, usually right before dinner. I spend 20 or 30 minutes planning my next day, enabling me to jump right in the following morning.

EMPIRE BUILDER EXERCISE

This evening, plan tomorrow today (PTT) by writing down your Daily 6, the key tasks you plan to accomplish tomorrow.

1.

2.

3.

4.

5.

6.

Check out how the BUILD system and Daily 6 can work together. Here's one of my journal entries.

If you use the PTT method, you'll always know what your next steps are. You will never wonder what to do. And if you follow the BUILD system, you also give yourself permission to *stop* working. Once you hit your Daily 6 and BUILD goals for the day, that's it. You are done. Give yourself the gift of time off, knowing you have already done everything you needed to do.

Maybe you work a full-time job. Maybe you're a single parent with kids. I totally get it, and that means your schedule won't look like mine. But that doesn't mean you won't be successful. If you have limited time, keep your BUILD goal as is, but reduce your Daily 6 to a Daily 3. I promise you will still leverage compound interest and build that empire.

CHAPTER 9

BUILD YOUR ECOMMERCE EMPIRE

Over the course of this book, you've learned how to build your own Ecommerce Empire with customized funnels to drive traffic that *you* control. You are on your way to building a seven-figure empire, because now you understand how to choose an IPO, structure your sales process, price your offers, and drive traffic to your site.

Remember that roadmap to seven figures? After you successfully build out sales funnel #1, you'll add #2, #3, and #4 to reach $1 Million!

#1. YOUR AWESOME PRODUCT

25 sales per day x $30 average cart = $750

#2. YOUR AWESOME PRODUCT

25 sales per day x $30 average cart = $750

#3. YOUR AWESOME PRODUCT

25 sales per day x $30 average cart = $750

#4. YOUR AWESOME PRODUCT

25 sales per day x $30 average cart = $750

Let's see how much you're doing in sales each day.

$$\$750 \times 4 = \$3,000$$

Now how many sales does that make for the year?

$$\$3,000 \times 365 = \$1,095,000$$

BOOM—you're there.

I hope I've proven to you that this goal is completely possible. But you also know that it is going to take some hard work to get there, even with the right strategy in place.

This journey is going to be tough. Most entrepreneurs don't succeed. But those who do reap massive rewards for themselves and their families.

The last thing I want you to consider is this:

Who do you want to become?

Who exactly is the New You—the entrepreneur who will build a massive Ecommerce Empire? Think about exactly what this New You will look like.

What time of day do they wake up?

Where do they live?

How do they spend their free time?

To truly succeed, you must clearly envision your future self and sincerely believe that you can and will become that person.

Because if you don't know who you want to become, how will you ever get there?

Remember that book I found from college with all of my goals listed out? I want to leave you with an even better version of that. For this final exercise, you're going to map out the New You.

EMPIRE BUILDER EXERCISE: MEET THE NEW YOU

This exercise gives you the chance to vividly fantasize about how amazing you life can become with your own Ecommerce Empire.

Do you want to live in a huge mansion? Buy a Porsche? Quit your day job? Travel the world?

Do you want to retire early? Perhaps even leave a legacy business for your family?

Most people set low expectations. But I want you to write down your wildest dreams here. If the idea of sharing them with others doesn't make you uncomfortable, then you aren't reaching far enough. Dig deep. Aim for the moon!

To help you envision this New You, complete the following worksheet.

The first set of questions will help you start dreaming big. The short-term goals will use the BUILD system. And the long-term goals will motivate you to keep building your empire. Have fun.

If money were no object…

How would you spend your free time?

Where would you live?

What would you look like?

What would you own?

Who would you learn from?

What will you achieve one week from today? (Add date on line below.)

[Hint: You can grab these from the Empire Builder Exercise you did in Chapter 8.]

By _____, I will…

B:

U:

I:

L:

D:

What will you achieve one month from today? (Add date on line below.)

By _____, I will…

B:

U:

I:

L:

D:

Here's who I will be in 1 year, on _____.

I am age:

My income is:

I work as a:

I look like this:

I live in this house:

I have these things:

I spend my time doing:

My relationship with this person is strong:

My Ecommerce Empire produces this much:

I have this amount saved for retirement:

Other goals:

Here's who I will be in 5 years, on _____.

I am age:

My income is:

I work as a:

I look like this:

I live in this house:

I have these things:

I spend my time doing:

My relationship with this person is strong:

My Ecommerce Empire produces this much:

I have this amount saved for retirement:

Other goals:

Here's who I will be in 10 years, on _____.

I am age:

My income is:

I work as a:

I look like this:

I live in this house:

I have these things:

I spend my time doing:

My relationship with this person is strong:

My Ecommerce Empire produces this much:

I have this amount saved for retirement:

Other goals:

You should return to these pages often. You might even want to take a screenshot so you can access it from your phone or tablet. Or make it into a poster to stick on your office wall.

And keep this book somewhere easy to find. When things get hard and you want to quit, I hope you'll come right back here and review what you wrote on these pages.

I know you can do this.

I truly believe that financial freedom through ecommerce is within your grasp, if you're just willing to reach for it.

CHAPTER 10

YOUR EMPIRE STARTS NOW

I want you to be part of the Ecommerce Empire Builder movement! To realize that every goal or dream you have for yourself, your family, and your business is 100% possible. And I want to help you every step of the way.

Reading this book was your first step in building your Ecommerce Empire. I congratulate you on getting to this stage, as most will not. The next step is implementing everything you have learned in a proven way.

To help with that, I'd like to provide you with some free additional bonuses and resources to put everything into practice.

- **6-Part FREE Sales Funnel Course:** Here I show you exactly how to build your business from scratch and, more importantly, how to launch it and bring in your first sales!
- **Sales Funnel Templates:** I will give you proven templates that our students have used to generate six- and seven-figure incomes. Download these templates with the click of a button and save time and money instead of designing your own.

- **Mindset & Goal Training:** You will also get private training and tracking sheets so you can crush your goals daily and develop a seven-figure mindset!

If you are ready to take action on what you learned, head over to...

EcommerceEmpireBuilders.com/kickstart, where you can access all of your free training. This link will ALWAYS be updated. No matter when you read this book, rest assured that all the training you implement is current with the tactics we are using at Ecommerce Empire Builders.

Your Empire Starts Now!

REFERENCES

"Fulfillment by Amazon." Amazon.com. https://sell.amazon.com/fulfillment-by-amazon.html.

Kulach, Karolina. "Alibaba: China's ecommerce giant highlighted." WebInterpret.com. November 8, 2017. https://www.webinterpret.com/us/blog/alibaba-chinas-e-commerce-giant-highlighted/.

Lajoie, Mark and Nick Shearman. "What Is Alibaba?" https://graphics.wsj.com/alibaba/.

Olson, Jeff. *The Slight Edge: Turning Simple Disciplines Into Massive Success & Happiness.* Greenleaf Book Group Press, 2013.

Otar, Chad. "What Percentage Of Small Businesses Fail—And How Can You Avoid Being One Of Them?" Forbes.com. October 25, 2018. https://www.forbes.com/sites/forbesfinancecouncil/2018/10/25/what-percentage-of-small-businesses-fail-and-how-can-you-avoid-being-one-of-them/?sh=7e3eff6643b5.

ACKNOWLEDGEMENTS

There are a TON of people I should thank for being so generous with their knowledge and sharing their business strategies with me—both those I've had the pleasure of meeting and others I've only been able to learn from within books.

First, and most importantly, I want to thank my wife Kellie for being there by my side for so many years of ups and downs in our businesses. Without your help every single day, there is no way I would have been able to accomplish what I have for us. I love you.

I'm beyond grateful for our community of Empire Builders. What first started as a side project and a way of sharing my ecommerce strategies with others quickly turned into an amazing movement that has impacted thousands of lives. I appreciate every single person who engages in our community and strives to take their business and life to the next level!

I want to thank some of the brilliant marketers and team members who helped me over the past 10 years or so, for not only sharing their ideas with me but also for being generous with their time.

Aliakbar Gulshan: For constantly pushing me out of my comfort zone, and taking the ideas I've had and skyrocketing them to the next level.

Jordan Strauss: Our copy chief at Ecommerce Empire Builders. Thanks for walking up to me at a small diner in Doylestown, PA, when you heard me talking my wife's ear off about paid advertising.

Julie Eason, Michelle Stampe, & Julie Willson from Thanet House Books: Thank you for helping me take what's in my brain and put it to paper. Also Julie W., thanks for saying hi at the airport. Otherwise this book would not have happened!

Dan Kennedy: Even though I've never met you in person, your books and courses gave me insights about business that I never knew even existed.

Lastly, I want to thank my entire team at Ecommerce Empire Builders for continuing to implement and stay on the cutting edge for all things ecommerce. Each of you has given me the chance to implement quickly and constantly push the limit in terms of what we do. I appreciate you all for showing up every single day.

Glossary

affiliate marketing: A type of marketing in which a business rewards one or more affiliates for each customer brought by the affiliate's own marketing efforts.

Alibaba: A Chinese multinational technology company specializing in ecommerce, retail, Internet, and technology.

AliExpress: An online retail service based in China owned by the Alibaba Group. Launched in 2010, it is made up of small businesses in China and other locations (such as Singapore) that offer products to international online buyers.

Amazon: A vast Internet-based enterprise that sells books, music, movies, housewares, electronics, toys, and many other goods, either directly or as the middleman between other retailers and Amazon.com's millions of customers.

Amazon FBA (Fulfillment by Amazon): An effective and reliable service that stores, packs, and ships orders. This service also handles returns and exchanges. Products are sent to Amazon's fulfillment centers and Amazon picks, packs, ships, and provides customer service for those products.

average cart value: A calculation featured in the stats area of your funnel. This calculation shows the average amount that is collected per customer throughout your entire funnel.

cold traffic: A group of prospective buyers who have never heard of your product or brand before.

complementary products: Products that are sold separately and often used together, each creating a demand for the other. For example, a tennis ball and a tennis racket.

continuity: A product or service you sell to your customer who buys or pays for it on a recurring basis, such as a subscription, single-use product, consumable product, or digital members area.

conversion rate: The number of conversions divided by the total number of visitors. For example, if an ecommerce site receives 200 visitors in a month and has 50 sales, the conversion rate would be 50 divided by 200, or 25 percent.

cost to acquire a customer: A metric used in ecommerce, the *cost to acquire a customer* is what you spend to get a customer to complete a purchase.

deep discount: A product offered in a sales funnel, the *deep discount* is an additional product or service offered at a much-reduced price to increase the total value of the sale.

digital product: A content-based or information product you offer as an upsell in your sales funnel that must usually only be created once, such as an e-book, FAQ sheet, "how-to" video, and so on.

direct competition: Other ecommerce businesses who sell products similar to yours or whose buyers are similar to yours.

downsell: An offer you make to the potential customer after they have declined your initial offer. As the name suggests, the former is a downgrade from the latter, with the idea being that the potential customer may be interested in a less expensive product.

dropshipping: A business model that makes you the intermediary between the supplier and the prospective buyer. You market and advertise the product, and the supplier handles fulfillment and shipping.

email marketing: An ecommerce sales strategy that involves promoting products via email to a list of subscribers.

Etsy: An online sales-and-marketing website that allows individuals and businesses to create digital storefronts to sell products online.

free + shipping: A marketing strategy where the seller offers an item or product and charges only a shipping fee to the buyer.

hot traffic: Prospective buyers who have bought from you before, who are most likely to know you, trust you, and therefore, buy from you again.

indirect competition: Other businesses who sell products or services related to those you sell, or who sell different products or services to the same buyers as you.

influencer marketing: A sales-and-promotion strategy that involves creating a relationship with a person or business that has a larger following than your own to get your product in front of a wider audience of potential buyers.

IPO (initial product offer): The main item the customer is buying in your funnel.

market: A broad category or industry. The main eight markets identified by Ecommerce Empire Builders include:

- beauty
- dating and relationships
- fitness
- health
- hobbies
- pets
- self-improvement
- weight loss

multi-product funnel: A sales funnel that guides buyers to purchase multiple products instead of just one.

niche: A smaller, more specific or specialized category within a market.

For example, within the health market, one may find several niches, such as herbal remedies, mental health, and supplements.

offer stack: The combination of many different products in order to increase both the perceived and actual value of the offer you are making. It's the reason someone will buy from you instead of your competition.

opt-in: The first step in a sales funnel. This is a page on a website where the buyer provides their email address or other contact information before proceeding to the completion of their order.

order bump: A sales-funnel feature that allows the buyer to pre-purchase an inexpensive additional item, usually related to the IPO.

order form: A page in the sales funnel where the buyer is prompted to select which item they would like to purchase and the number of units they want. Shipping and billing information is collected here.

paid advertising: Platforms a seller can utilize to market their products for a fee, such as Facebook Ads and Google Ads.

physical product: Any material item you can touch, see, and ship (as opposed to a digital or info product).

quantity breaks/quantity break discounts: A discount offered to your customers when they buy more than one of any item. The more they buy, the more they save.

sales funnel: A web page designed to lead a prospective buyer to a sale. Basic components include an opt-in/sales page, order form with quantity breaks, order bumps, multiple upsells, and a thank-you page.

sales page: The first page of a sales funnel. The sales page collects the prospective buyer's contact information (usually an email address).

Shopify: An online sales-and-marketing website that allows individuals and businesses to create digital storefronts to sell products online.

single-product funnel: A sales funnel that sells only one product.

subniche: Smaller, more specialized categories within a niche. For example, within the herbal remedies niche, subniches might include (but would not be limited to) organic cold remedies for children, tea for lowering blood sugar, or essential oils for mothers who are breastfeeding.

subscription: A service or recurring sale that a buyer signs up for or opts into. This can include recurring deliveries of physical products; recurring delivery of digital/information products; or membership in a specific community or interest group.

thank-you page: The final page of a sales funnel, thanking the customer for their purchase and usually offering them another opportunity to make an additional purchase.

unbeatable offer: This is usually the seller's main product as well as one or two additional items that are perceived as high value to the customer while being low cost to the seller.

upsell: An item, product, subscription, or service offered to the prospective buyer in order to generate more revenue for the business.

warm traffic: Prospective buyers who may be familiar with you but have not bought from you yet. For example, if an influencer promotes your product to their audience, the audience is then warm traffic for you.

ABOUT THE AUTHOR

Peter Pru has been involved in internet marketing for more than 10 years, with experience in affiliate marketing, agency work, and ecommerce. He is the founder and CEO of Ecommerce Empire Builders, where he shares his tactics and strategies for building wildly profitable ecommerce businesses from scratch. His training has been featured in *Forbes*, *Entrepreneur*, and many other publications. He is also the founder and CEO of Untapped Supplements, the first all-natural supplement brand designed specifically for entrepreneurs and high-performers.

An early pioneer in online ecommerce education, Peter has produced content that has been viewed over five million times. More than 10,000 people have taken his online training programs. He is one of the leading authorities in ecommerce and sales funnels. Peter currently resides with his family in the suburbs of Philadelphia.

Connect with him at PeterPru.com.

Index

Numbers

$1 million, reaching, 155–156
1-year projection, 160
1.6 benchmark for pricing, 121–122
5-year projection, 161
10-year projection, 162
100% satisfaction, offering, 131

A

achievements, setting goals for, 159
action, taking, 12
ad example, 131. *See also* paid advertising
adjusting prices, 121
advertising platforms, 143
affiliate marketplaces, 119, 135
affirmations, repeating, 16
The Alibaba Group, 65, 68, 72–73. *See also* sourcing products
AliExpress limitations of, 72–73

pricing example, 73
services provided by, 68
Amazon
proving products on, 50–56
star ratings, 53
using as research tool, 50
Amazon Associates, 119
Amazon's FBA (Fulfillment by Amazon), 65, 79

B

Bark Box, 111
Best Sellers Rank on Amazon, 53
blogs, checking out, 37
body
in BUILD system, 147
disconnect with mind, 12–13
broken or lost items, 113
BUILD system. *See also* workflow
body, 147
Daily 6 and PTT (Plan Tomorrow Today), 153

development, 148
income, 148
potential of, 149
relationships, 148
you, 148
businesses, failure of, 10
business-integrated lifestyle, 29
Buyers List, 145

C

challenges, stacking with habits, 15
choices, failure of, 11
clickable images, including, 119
ClickBank, 119
cold shower, taking, 14
cold traffic, 133
collectibles, 113
communities, creating, 116
company logo, posting, 137
competition
  identifying, 35, 40
  and niches, 31
complementary products, 94–95, 98, 104, 117–118. See also products
consumable products, 112. See also products
content, sharing on social media, 138

Continuity Buyers List, 145–146
continuity upsells, 94, 98, 110–117
control
  implementing, 8
  importance of, 13
credibility, establishing, 108, 126–128, 132
custom audiences, 142
Customer Reviews on Amazon, 53–54
customer service support, 128
customers. *See also* lookalike audiences; testimonials and reviews
  considering and helping, 27, 34
  identifying, 35
  identifying desires of, 36
  learning about, 37–43

D

Daily 6 and PTT (Plan Tomorrow Today), 151–154. *See also* workflow
daily challenges, following for week, 13–16
daily sales, calculating, 156
daily workout, adding five minutes to, 14

deep discounts, 58, 93–94, 97, 101–104, 109–110
delivery, confirming, 95
desires of customers
　identifying, 36, 41, 43
　versus wants, 43
development in BUILD system, 148
discomfort, adjusting to, 13
Dollar Shave Club, 111, 116
dropshipping, 66–69, 72–73

E

EcommerceEmpireBuilders.com/kickstart, 80, 166
email marketing, 92, 134, 144–145
emotion, appealing to, 128–129, 132
Empire Builder Exercises
　Amazon research, 53
　BUILD system, 150
　building continuity, 114
　complementary products, 104
　credibility, 132
　Daily 6 and PTT (Plan Tomorrow Today), 152
　daily challenges, 16
　emotion, 132
　legacy, 9

listing products, 49
logic, 132
markets and niches, 24, 30
New You, 158
"Niche Research" folder, 35
niches and subniches, 30
offers and products for IPO, 62–63
people in niches, 34
price comparisons, 69
social media, 139
suppliers, 75
vetting suppliers, 72
Etsy, 79
experience of suppliers, noting, 70

F

F+S, 56–58, 101–104
Facebook, posting on, 138
Facebook groups, 37–38, 119
failure of businesses, 10
　fear of, 33
　learning from, 11
features, including, 128
feedback loops and resistance, 10–12
Fiverr, 106
followers, finding, 138
food, varying, 14

Free-Plus-Shipping, 56–58, 101–104
Frequently bought together products on Amazon, 52
friends and family, reaching out to, 140
front-end offer, pricing, 74
funnel. *See* sales funnels

G
goals, setting, 159
group access, 113–114, 117
Gulshan, Aliakbar, 78–80

H
habit stacking, 15
hot traffic, 133

I
images and video, 106. *See also* product images
income in BUILD system, 148
indirect competition, identifying, 35, 40
influencers identifying, 35, 39–40, 140–141
paying, 135, 138–139
information products, 108, 113, 115. *See also* products
Inner Circle program, 78
Instagram, 38, 138

IPO (initial product offer)
characteristics of, 63
determining, 46–50
displaying on order page, 93
irresistible offers, 125–126

L
legacy exercise, 9
lifestyle images, 106
limited-time offer, 59. *See also* offers
lingo, noting and learning, 36, 41–42
logic, appealing to, 130–132
logo, posting, 137
lookalike audiences, 143–144. *See also* customers
lost or broken items, 113
lowering prices, 121

M
mail, sending products by, 115
manufacturers and trading companies, 71
margins, considering, 122
markets and niches, 20–30
master and puppet, 12–18
Master Bucket List, 146
metrics, watching, 120–123
mind, disconnect with from body, 12

MIND in control, 17
Mindset & Goal Training, 166
mindset of Empire Builder
  peers, 7
  routines and habits, 6
  self-empowerment, 7–9
  self-reliance, 6
mix and match, 61, 96, 100. See also offers
money-back guarantee, offering, 126, 131
multi-product funnels, 82–86

N

New Releases And Most Wished For on Amazon, 54
New You, 6–7, 11, 17, 156–158. See also you in BUILD system
"Niche Research" folder, creating, 35
niches
  becoming observer in, 32
  determining desires of, 41
  finding problems in, 32–33
  identifying, 19–20
  and IPO (initial product offer), 47
  learning about, 37–43
  and markets, 20–30
  problems and solutions, 28
  subniches, 25
  trends in, 35
  uncovering, 31–32
no, saying, 14
numbers, watching, 120–123

O

observer in niche, becoming, 32
offers. See also limited-time offer; mix and match; testers needed; unbeatable offers
  combining, 61
  linking to, 95
online forums, 39
opportunities finding, 42
  offering, 116
opt-in/sales page, 89, 92, 96, 105–108
order page + order bump, 89, 92–93, 95–96, 108–109

P

package offer, 95, 97, 99
paid advertising, 135, 141–144. See also ad example
paid influencers, 135
payment gateways, 109
PayPal, 109

percent to a cause, 59–60
photos, using, 106. *See also* product images
Pinterest, checking out, 38
pixel id, 141–142
posting to social media, 137–138
price
    adjusting, 121
    displaying on order page, 93
    and F+S, 102
    of products on Amazon, 52
    and sales funnels, 81
    understanding, 73–75
problems. *See also* solving problems
    and complaints, 36, 42
    finding in niches, 32–33
    and solutions, 28
Product Categories on Amazon, 51–52
product images, using to establish credibility, 127–128. *See also* images and video
Product Information on Amazon, 53
product reviews
    posting, 126–127
    reading, 70
product testers clubs, 114
Product Type on Amazon, 51

products. *See also* complementary products; consumable products; information products; sourcing products
    choosing, 45–46
    frequently bought together on Amazon, 52
    increasing perceived value of, 115
    IPO (initial product offer), 46–50
    proving, 50–58
    refilling and replacing, 113
    single use, 113
products purchased, analyzing, 32
profile, creating for social media, 137
prospects, retargeting, 142–143
proving products, 50–58
PTT (Plan Tomorrow Today), 151–154
puppet and master, 12–18

R

rankings, checking for suppliers, 70
Reddit groups, checking out, 38–39
relationships in BUILD system, 148

replacing items, 113
research
    Empire Builder Exercise, 55
    importance of, 31
resistance and feedback loops, 10–12
response rate, checking for suppliers, 71
retargeting prospects, 142–143
reviews and testimonials, 107

S

sale price, considering, 74–75
sales, resistance free, 81–82
sales angles, 56, 105
sales copy, 105–106
sales funnels
    advantages, 100
    average cart values, 83–85
    binary choices, 104
    choosing platforms, 80–82
    considering changes to, 122
    cost to acquire products, 85–86
    daily goal, 122–123
    designing, 77–80
    driving traffic to, 123
    ecosystem and business fundamentals, 101, 103
    free course, 165
    fundamentals, 86–89
    goal of, 104
    integrating unbeatable offers, 101–104
    multiple products, 82–86
    opt-in/sales page, 89, 92, 96, 105–108
    order page + order bump, 89, 92–93, 96, 108–109
    templates, 165
    testing, 123
    thank-you page, 91, 95, 99, 118–120
    tracking, 120–123
    upsells, 90–91, 93–95, 97–99, 109–118
    using, 80
self-empowerment, 7–9
self-reliance, 6
selling. *See* traffic
Shopify, 78–80
showering, 14
single-use products, 113
social media, 136–140
solving problems, 29, 31. *See also* problems and solutions
sourcing products. *See also* The Alibaba Group; products
    dropshipping, 66–69
    understanding price, 73–75
stacking, practicing, 15
Stripe, 109

subniches, 25
subscribe-and-save model,
  115–116
subscription services, 111,
  114–115
success, envisioning, 157
suppliers and dropshipping,
  68–69
vetting, 70–72

T

tagging on social sites, 138
Take Action-Measure-Analyze-
  Adjust-Repeat, 12
Testers Clubs, 116
testers needed, 60–61. *See also*
  offers
testimonials and reviews, 107,
  126–127. *See also* customers
thank-you page, 91, 95, 99,
  118–120
tracking sales funnels,
  120–123
trading companies and
  manufacturers, 71
traffic
  Buyers List, 145
  cold, warm, and hot, 133
  Continuity Buyers List,
    145–146
  controlling, 134–135
  credibility, 126–128

driving to funnels, 123
earning, 133–136
email marketing, 144–145
emotion, 128–129
friends and family, 140
influencers, 140–141
irresistible offers, 125–126
logic, 130–131
Master Bucket List, 146
not controlled, 134, 136
overview, 125–126
owning, 133–135
paid advertising, 141–144
social media, 136–140
Welcome Series list, 145
trends in niches, noticing,
  35–36, 40–41
trials, offering, 117

U

unbeatable offers, 56, 101–104.
  See also offers
uncomfortable, being, 13, 16
upsells
  complementary products,
    117–118
  continuity, 110–117
  deep discounts, 109–110
  mixing and matching, 100
  sales funnels, 90–91,
    93–95, 97–99
  sequence of, 112

V

vernacular, noting, 36
video and images, 106

W

waking up early, 12–13
wants versus desires, 43
warm traffic, 133
week-long training, 13–15
Welcome Series list, 145

"While supplies last," 105–106
workflow, managing, 147. *See also* BUILD system; Daily 6 and PTT (Plan Tomorrow Today)

Y

you in BUILD system, 148. *See also* New You
YouTube, 39, 80